SIR THOM

CW00448336

Scholar, Statesman and Son of Saffron Walden

SWHS PUBLICATIONS

SIR THOMAS SMITH

Scholar, Statesman and Son of Saffron Walden

Jeremy Collingwood

SWHS Publications

SERIES EDITOR JACQUELINE COOPER

To Margaret for fifty golden years

Other publications by Saffron Walden Historical Society:

Ward, Jennifer C., *The De Bohun Charter of Saffron Walden* (1986)
Saffron Walden History (Journal: 1972-1991)
Saffron Walden Historical Journal (2001- 2012 ongoing)
Ball, Geoffrey., *Land, Agriculture & Industry* (2010)
White, Malcolm, *The Place Names of Saffron Walden* (2011)

Other publications by Jeremy Collingwood:

Francis Paynter: a remarkable Guildfordian (undated)
The Criminal Law of East and Central Africa (1967)
Hannah More - with Margaret Collingwood (1990)
As a Witness to the Light: the story of Chengelo School in Zambia (2006)
Mr. Saffron Walden: the life and times of George Stacey Gibson 1818-1883 (2008)
A Lakeland Saga: the story of the Collingwood and Altounyan Family in Coniston and Aleppo (2012)

© Jeremy Collingwood & Saffron Walden Historical Society 2012

ISBN 978-1-873669-08-2

Published by SWHS Publications

Hon. Editor: 24 Pelham Road, Clavering, Essex CB11 4PQ, England.

Contents

Note: the origins of the chapter sub-titles can be found in the text of the chapter concerned.

List of Illustrations

We are very grateful to Gordon Ridgewell for photographing many of the images, also for permission to use these images by courtesy of Saffron Walden Town Library Committee and Essex County Council, Trustees of Saffron Walden Town Library. Image nos 2, 3, 4, 6, 7, 25, 33, 35, 40 & 46 are from the Cliff Stacey Album Vol 1 in the Town Library. Image nos 10, 11, 13, 17, 18, 19, 20, 21, 23, 24, 27 & 28 are from Granger, J., *History of England with Portraits* Vol 3 in the Town Library. Image nos 36, 37, 38, 39, 41 & 42 are by Margaret Collingwood. Further acknowledgements as below.

30. Title page *De Republica Anglorum* 1583. Reproduced by courtesy of Saffron Walden Town Library.

31. The Procession of the Knights of the Garter 1576 by M. Gheeraerts. © National Portrait Gallery, London.

32. Sir Francis Walsingham. © National Portrait Gallery, London.

33. Gabriel Harvey.

34. Detail from map by Boazio 1599, showing Sir Thomas Smith's proposed Irish Colony in the Arde. Image by courtesy of Mark Thompson.

35. The Close, Saffron Walden.

36. Hill Hall south range.

37. Hill Hall inner courtyard.

38. Hill Hall Tudor fireplace.

39. Bust of Sir Thomas Smith at Hill Hall.

40. Smith's coat of arms on Saffron Walden Charter.

41. St Michael's Church, Theydon Mount.

42. Tomb of Sir Thomas Smith at St Michael's Church, Theydon Mount.

43. Portrait of Sir Thomas Smith at Saffron Walden Town Hall. Photograph David Whorlow by courtesy of Saffron Walden Town Council.

44. The many faces of Sir Thomas Smith.

45. Thomas Smith globe. By courtesy Queens' College Library, Cambridge.

46. Battle Ditches, Saffron Walden.

Editor's Preface

This volume is the third in a new series of local history books, the SWHS Publications. This series is sponsored by the Saffron Walden Historical Society, publishers of the *Saffron Walden Historical Journal*. In common with the *Journal*, SWHS Publications aims to bring into the public domain works of original research which are worthy of wider readership, and which relate to the history of North-west Essex. Each volume will be a quality production, but modestly priced with a limited print run, and non-profit-making. The contributions of author and editor are freely given, so that all income can be devoted to future publications. We hope by this means to add to published material on the history of this area, either from the fruits of new research, or to bring to light other works of history long out-of-print and worthy of reproduction. Previous titles in the series (Geoffrey Ball's *Land, Agriculture and Industry*, and Malcolm White's *The Place Names of Saffron Walden*) have reflected on the historic importance of local agriculture, and on the amount of history to be found in local street names. The current volume, the first biographical portrait in the series, offers a summary of the life of one of the town's most famous sons, and is particularly timely since the 500th anniversary of Sir Thomas Smith's birth in Saffron Walden is imminent.

The Author

After graduating from Corpus Christi, Cambridge, Jeremy Collingwood taught Law in Zambia and then worked for the Director of Public Prosecutions in London. He was later ordained into the Anglican ministry, holding incumbencies in Bristol and Guildford before retirement. This is his seventh book, previous publications including *Mr. Saffron Walden: the life and times of George Stacey Gibson 1818-1883*; and, most recently, *A Lakeland Saga: the story of the Collingwood and Altounyan Family in Coniston and Aleppo*, which features the real lives of the children featuring in Arthur Ransome's Swallows and Amazons saga. Living in Saffron Walden with his wife Margaret, he continues to act as a retired minister in the town's team ministry, studying local history and supporting several local organisations including the Saffron Walden Historical Society.

Jacqueline Cooper
Hon. Editor, SWHS Publications

Foreword

In this latest account of Sir Thomas Smith's life and work, Jeremy Collingwood poses again the question of why this significant Elizabethan scholar and statesman is hardly known among the people of the most charming town in Essex. He was born in that town, Saffron Walden, probably in 1514. The most plausible answer is that the fields in which he engaged – and he did so brilliantly if somewhat erratically – are not those to which people in general readily respond. So it is timely and appropriate that the Saffron Walden Historical Society should now add this study to its developing publications programme. Readers coming fresh to this intriguing strand in the annals of the Elizabethan era will find the author's depiction of the contextual political and historical background helpful and informative. Of course, any account of Sir Thomas Smith and his work is essentially also an important aspect of the story of Hill Hall at Theydon Mount. Smith himself, drawing on his continental experience, inspired the innovative architectural features of the building which make it of such significance in the development of English architecture. As such it is Smith's most conspicuous monument in Essex and redolent of his remarkable life and work.

Prominent among the heraldic devices in the Smyth – as the name became among his descendants – coat-of-arms is that of a supporting salamander, the mythical creature that reputedly survives in fire and flame. It is appropriately symbolic of the vicissitudes of Smith's own life and career. It is all part of the enigmas that remain in evaluating this Elizabethan scholar's life. Jeremy Collingwood's essay will not be the last account of this absorbing character's life but it will find a valid place in the now considerable Smith bibliography. It is probable that the remaining enigmatic episodes in the Smith experience will never be fully resolved unless, which is unlikely, further source material becomes available for historians to evaluate.

It would be very satisfying if this latest reminder of the importance of Smith led to a permanent and accessible presentation in Saffron Walden of his roles and purposes in all their complicated variety. All that took place in the most inspiring and perhaps formative reign in our country's history. An article in the Penny Magazine of 1845 stated that Smith was 'no ordinary personage'. It would be difficult to define him more succinctly than that. Those who read and enjoy this book should be profitably tempted to explore the other relevant publications that record this man and his experience in and out of favour with the great Queen it was his duty to serve.

His home, Hill Hall, was almost entirely destroyed, though now restored by English Heritage, by a disastrous fire in 1968 which was started by spontaneous combustion in the roof timbers. His parish church, St Michael the Archangel, was also largely destroyed by fire having been struck by lighting it is said, but restored in 1611. Within the church there is an arched monument to Smith. His recumbent effigy lies within the recess with a flame-girt salamander at his feet. Inscribed around the frame of the arch are the words: 'What yearth (*sic*) or sea or skies conteyne what creatures in them be my mynde (*sic*) did seeke to know my soule the heavens continually.' This, an apt summation of Smith's intellectual attributes and religious beliefs which with the salamander characterise the man who is the absorbing subject of Jeremy Collingwood's book.

Kenneth Neale
President, The Saffron Walden Historical Society

Introduction

Sir Thomas Smith can justly claim to be one of Saffron Walden's most distinguished sons. It is right and proper that in the Council Chamber of the Town Hall his portrait sits centrally over the mantelpiece, where he is supported on one side by George Stacey Gibson, the town's greatest philanthropist, and on the other by Gibson's wife, Elizabeth Tuke Gibson. Yet outside the ranks of the cognoscenti Smith is hardly known today in his native town. Smith's curriculum vitae speaks for itself. He was the first Regius Professor of Civil Law at Cambridge, Vice-Chancellor of Cambridge University, Provost of Eton, Principal Secretary of State to Edward VI and Elizabeth I, a Member of Parliament under the last three Tudor monarchs, several times ambassador to France and the Low Countries, a Privy Councillor, Chancellor of the Order of the Garter, and not least the builder of Hill Hall, one of England's first great classical or Paladian mansions. He was also the author of two of the most eminent writings of Tudor times, *The Discourse of the Commonweal*, 1549, described by Ian Archer as 'the most impressive piece of economic analysis produced in the sixteenth century' (*The Oxford Dictionary of National Biography*, OUP, 2004-10); and *De Republica Anglorum*, 1562-1565, an authoritative account of the English constitution and legal system. Professor Maitland, the legal historian, said that nobody should think of writing about Elizabethan England without taking account of Smith's book. It should also be mentioned that Smith was one of the great letter writers of his age, and nearly 700 of his letters survive.

What sort of a man was Smith? In many ways he was not untypical of his age: a self-made man who in a time of unprecedented religious and political ferment rose from obscurity to achieve riches and power. He climbed up the greasy pole of social advancement through his undoubted intellect and a large measure of good fortune. That good fortune included his capacity to make very successful marriages. His two wives, Elizabeth Carkeke and Philippa, Lady Hampden, both brought wealth and lands into Smith's possession. Without their assets Smith could never have built his great mansion at Hill Hall. Smith was also fortunate in his friends, many of them from his Cambridge days. His friendship with men like John Cheke and Roger Ascham was to bring him to the attention of powerful people in royal circles. His fall from grace during the rule of Northumberland worked in his favour under the reign of Queen Mary. His low profile helped Smith to keep his head. He was slow to be rehabilitated under Elizabeth, but his restoration and subsequent promotion owed a great deal to the steadfast friendship of William Cecil, Lord Burghley.

Smith was not a natural courtier. As he himself recognised he was too quick to express his opinion in robust and undiplomatic terms. He admitted 'My fault is plainness and that I cannot dissemble enmity or pleasure'. He seemed to be awkward in the presence of women and lacked the oleaginous skills to woo or flatter them. Under the Protectorate he incurred the dangerous hostility of the Duchess of Somerset, and under Elizabeth sought to badger the Queen into marriage. He was too prone to hector his wives and enjoyed a fractious relationship with them. For a person well grounded in reality, Smith showed an extraordinary naivety in his speculative ventures in copper production and in Irish colonisation.

Both ventures brought him much heartache and loss. He was unfortunate in having no legitimate children, only a son, born out of wedlock, Thomas junior, who proved a big disappointment to his father. In many ways he might have been happier if he had remained within academic circles where his intellectual star was readily recognised.

Despite leaving Saffron Walden for Cambridge as a young boy, Smith did not forget his native town. Smith's brother, John, remained in Saffron Walden and became active in the town's affairs. Sir Thomas Smith played a part in obtaining the new charter of the town in 1549, when his brother, John, became the first Treasurer. Smith was responsible for obtaining letters patent for the re-founding of the Almshouses under the name of the King Edward VI's Almshouses. He also obtained a new charter for the school, which became one of eighteen King Edward VI grammar schools in the country. Towards the end of his life Smith established two scholarships and two fellowships at Queens' College Cambridge for which his own relatives or scholars of Walden School were to be given priority. In his will Smith provided that a clever child, the son of one of his servants, was to have five marks a year to keep him at Walden School and then to go up to Cambridge. He presented his native town with a large silver cup. Smith took a close interest in the career of Gabriel Harvey, the Saffron Walden born scholar and did everything to encourage the young writer. So if only for these reasons alone, Saffron Walden should be proud of Thomas Smith and, as we approach the 500th anniversary of his birth, give him the honour that his achievements deserve.

Acknowledgements

This book was written out of a simple conviction that Sir Thomas Smith ought to be better known in his native town, where his name normally evinces a look of blank ignorance. I have sought to write a straight-forward account building on the two biographies of Smith – that of John Strype which came out in 1698, and especially the serious academic study by Mary Dewar, which was published in 1964, and to which I am much indebted. It was a joy to do a lot of the research in the excellent Town Library, where I was given every assistance by Jill Palmer, the librarian, and her staff. Dr Tim Egginton, the Librarian of Queens' College, Cambridge, was kind enough to show me the College library and dining hall and sent me the photographs of the old library and Smith's globe. Martyn Everett was a great source of knowledge and inspiration. I am most grateful to Kenneth Neale, who has written and lectured on Thomas Smith, for his Foreword. The photography of Gordon Ridgewell is a marvellous asset to any book, and I am most thankful for his help. But my greatest debt is owed to Jacqueline Cooper, the General Editor of the Series, who has been encouraging and resourceful, and without whose assiduous labours this book would not have seen the light of day. But I must accept the full responsibility for any errors or omissions that the careful reader will discover.

Jeremy Collingwood

The tomb of Sir Thomas Smith at St Michael's Church, Theydon Mount, Essex. Below, one of the murals at his home, Hill Hall, Essex, depicting Cupid and Psyche.

1
The Lonely Boy

'Tho' he sometimes fell, he fell softly, and fell to rise again with more glory'

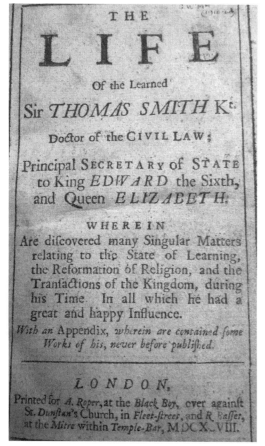

THE
LIFE
Of the Learned
Sir *THOMAS SMITH* Kt.
Doctor of the CIVIL LAW;

Principal SECRETARY of STATE
to King *EDWARD* the Sixth,
and Queen *ELIZABETH*.

WHEREIN

Are discovered many Singular Matters
relating to the State of Learning,
the Reformation of Religion, and the
Transactions of the Kingdom, during
his Time. In all which he had a
great and happy Influence.

With an Appendix, *wherein are contained some
Works of his, never before published.*

LONDON,
Printed for *A. Roper*, at the *Black Boy*, over against
St. *Dunstan's* Church, in *Fleet-street*, and *R. basset*,
at the *Mitre* within *Temple-Bar*, MDCXLVIII.

John Strype's Dedicatory - to Sir Edward Smith of Hill Hall in Essex, Baronet.

'He was a person that lived in very critical times, occasioned by court factions, and the frequent alterations of religion, and the various dispositions and interests of the Princes whom he served. So that he could hardly keep himself always upon his legs; but by his great wisdom and moderation, tho' he sometimes fell, he fell softly, and fell to rise again with more glory.'

'Your said ancestor, Sir, was the best scholar in his time, a most admirable philosopher, orator, linguist and moralist. And from whence it came to pass, that he was also a very wise statesman, and a person withal of most unalterable integrity and justice ... and lastly, a constant embracer of the Reformed religion, and therein made a holy and good end.' *The Life of the Learned Sir Thomas Smith Kt.* by John Strype (1698).

Fig 1. Title page of John Strype's biography of Sir Thomas Smith, a copy of which is in Saffron Walden Town Library.

The Tudors saw the emergence of England out of the feudal period and the fratricidal Wars of the Roses into a brave new world dominated by powerful rulers and ambitious courtiers. It was a dangerous world in which those at the centre of power could as easily lose their heads as make a fortune. It was a turbulent world riven by religious disputes as Protestantism arose to challenge the pre-eminence of the Roman Catholic Church. Society was much shaken and reshaped. The enclosure of land by wealthy landlords to make space for sheep deprived many poor people of common land for growing their crops or grazing their animals, and cast them adrift as a displaced peasantry. Furthermore the efforts of the monarch to raise money for foreign and domestic enterprises by debasing the coinage led to inflation. Enclosure and inflation and religious discontent were a constant threat to the peace and good order of the nation. This was the background to the life of Sir Thomas Smith. It was remarkable in such critical times that he kept his head and although he sometimes fell he managed to get back on his feet again despite all his personal and political vicissitudes.

Sir Thomas Smith rose to hold one of the great offices of state, Secretary of State first to King Edward VI and then to Queen Elizabeth 1. But he did not come from one of the great families of the land. His first biographer, John Strype, described Smith's father as a gentleman of 'good rank, quality and wealth', as the owner of property in Essex, London and Somerset, and as High Sheriff of Essex and Hertford in 1539 (Fig. 1).[1] This is all denied by Smith's later biographer, Mary Dewar, although the High Sheriff of Hertfordshire and Essex in 1539, was in fact one John Smith. Whether this was our man's father must remain conjectural. The town has intriguing references to a John Smith, hosier and churchwarden, who held property at Horn Lane in the town and John Smith of Market End, tailor and regrator of ale, in the 1440s, but it is not known whether they were connected.[2] What we can say is that the Smith family was among the more prominent members of the town of Saffron Walden. We know that Thomas Smith's brother was treasurer to the town and a member of the Corporation, and therefore probably sufficiently well off to pay tax. One researcher puts the case succinctly:

In 1549 sixty-two members of the town were assessed for taxation, of whom twenty-five were rated at twenty shillings or more. Of these twenty-five, no less than seventeen appear as members of the corporation – yet of the assistants only one, John Cotton, has the designation of "gentleman". The rest were yeomen, men of substance, farming land around Walden and living in the town, their prosperity deriving from the fertility of the countryside.[3]

Fig. 2. Saffron Walden Church with lantern spire.

Saffron Walden was first known as *Wealadenu*, meaning 'the valley of the Britons or serfs' in Old English. It was later known as Chipping (or Market) Walden being a strategically placed market town for the Uttlesford Hundred in north-west Essex. The town had grown up around the church and castle on Bury Hill and the market square with its medieval shopping 'rows' lying to the south of the church. From around the time of Richard II in the late 14th century, the saffron plant was grown on the chalky soils around the town for some three to four hundred years, and the town changed its name to Saffron Walden. In the 1549 charter the seal of the town showed 'walls with four towers, gateway and portcullis enclosing three saffron flowers'. William Camden, the Tudor historian, wrote of Walden that 'the fieldes on every side look pleasant with saffron'. On her progress through the district Queen Elizabeth was presented by the mayor with a pound weight of saffron.

Thomas Smith described himself as a solitary boy, one much given to ill health and introspection. As he wandered the fields of saffron, barley and sheep around his native town he would have looked down on the distinctive lantern on top of the tower of the church of St Mary the Virgin, for the town lies in a hollow (Fig. 2). As someone who was to take a great interest in architecture, the young boy would doubtless have been greatly impressed by the rebuilding in the Perpendicular style of the aisles and nave of his parish church. Much of this work was undertaken under the supervision of the great master-mason and architect, John Wastell (*c.*1460–*c.*1515), who left his mark on the Abbey Church of Bury St Edmunds, Great St Mary and King's College Chapel in Cambridge, and elsewhere.

The small community of Saffron Walden had been dominated for centuries by the Benedictine Abbey of Walden, which lay a mile to the west of the town. The monastery was founded as a priory by Geoffrey de Mandeville, Earl of Essex, in 1136, although this date is disputed. When Thomas Smith was a boy the Abbey was in decline. Thomas Cromwell's visitor, John ap Rice, reported to his master in October 1535 that 'there are now only seven persons left, and they are very old; [he] had so persuaded them in [his] lecture which [he] kept daily among them that there was no sanctity in monkery. You might soon have the house abandoned if you would.'[4] Furthermore the Abbot, Robert Baryngton, confided to ap Rice that he had secretly contracted marriage. Probably as a result of this scandal, Baryngton resigned or was removed and the Abbey was granted to William More, the suffragan of Colchester, to hold *in commendam* (i.e. it was commended to the care of the bishop pending the appointment of a pastor). On 22 March 1538 the monastery and its extensive possessions in England surrendered to the King. Five days later the whole estate, with a net value of £372 18s 1d, a huge sum, was granted to the Lord Chancellor, Sir Thomas Audley, in fee simple. Overnight at the stroke of a pen the institution which had held the town in its sway for 400 years was transferred from monastic to secular hands. It could have caused a revolution but as far as history records it passed with hardly a whimper.

From 1514 Saffron Walden was administered by the Guild of the Holy Trinity, which combined the role of a chantry chapel saying masses for the souls of its founders, as well as exercising local government powers and running the local school. In 1547 all chantries, including the Guild of the Holy Trinity, were abolished and their lands were forfeited to the Crown. According to Strype, John Smith, the father of Thomas, paid the enormous sum of £531 14s 11d to buy back for the town the lands formerly belonging to the Guild. But Dewar says the payment was not by Smith's father but by Smith's elder brother when Thomas' rising fortunes as Secretary had made the family more prosperous. In any event the town was able to obtain a new charter, dated 1 February 1549, with a council of 24 members of 'the most honest and discreet men'. The charter also granted to the town the market, two mills, the right to hold a Lent Fair, the Court of Pie Powder and the right to hold a court once in three weeks for the recovery of small debts.[5] John Smith the Younger is named in the charter as the 'first and present treasurer'. Strype says that brother John Smith was 'the chief instrument and procurer of the new erection of the Corporation of the Town of Walden in 1549.[6] The charter has the royal emblems of the Crown, the Tudor Rose, the Fleur de Lis, and the Portcullis, along its top (Fig. 3). Significantly it also bears the coat of arms of Sir Thomas Smith, which testifies to the leading role that he played in its granting.[7] There is an amusing entry in the Corporation Account Book: 'To Mr Secretary Smythe in rewarde, one dozen larkes, 2/-.[8] When Elizabeth came to the throne it was Smith, assisted by his cousin George Nicholls, the Recorder, who administered to the Treasurer and Chamberlains the oaths of loyalty to the new Queen.

Fig. 3. Saffron Walden Charter 1549, with Sir Thomas Smith's coat-of-arms, reflecting his crucial role in obtaining the charter for the town.

King Edward's charter gave the new corporation power to administer and maintain the almshouse and the grammar school provided they included the name of Edward VI in their titles. John Smith the Younger also played a big part in saving the Abbey Lane almshouses (Fig. 4). These almshouses were founded in the early 15th century by the Guild of our Lady of Pity. The old Guild was dissolved in 1547. It seems that it was John who persuaded Thomas, as Secretary of State, to obtain letters patent from the King to re-found the almshouses under the name of King Edward's Almshouse. Smith's father and uncle became joint keepers of the Almshouse, and their family friend, William Strachey, was the first chamberlain.[9] The town fathers specifically acknowledged that in obtaining these privileges 'God had called to their aid a good soliciter in a position of authority, one Sir Thomas Smyth, Knight, brother of John Smyth the younger, and one of the King's principal Secretaries'.[10]

Fig. 4. Chapel of the medieval Almshouses (later demolished), which were re-founded with the help of John Smith and his Secretary of State brother, Thomas, in 1549.

According to his own autobiography Thomas was born on the 23 December 1513, the second son of John Smith, described in local land deeds as a draper.[11] However, the astrological table in Smith's Memoirs suggest that he was born a year later on 23 December 1514.[12] John Smith, the father, owned two small fields of meadow and pasture, probably for sheep, and one larger field on which he grew saffron, and is supposed to have lived in a house in the north-east corner of the Market Square (Fig. 5). There are also said to have been connections with the Priory and what is now called Emson Close (Figs. 6,7).[13]

It would also seem that John Smith senior had larger landholdings although this is not certain. Smith's mother, Agnes Charnock, was of Lancastrian origins. Thomas had two brothers, the eldest, John, followed his father as a draper, whilst the youngest brother, George, went to London and became a prosperous merchant and member of the Draper's Company. The Draper's Company was an association of wool and cloth merchants and was one of the most powerful trade guilds in the City of London. There were also four sisters, Agnes, Margery, Alice and Jane, of whom the last two were married (see family tree below). Later Thomas would look after John's children and grandchildren and those of one of his sisters. As we have seen brother John Smith was the first Treasurer of the new commonalty or council established under the 1549 charter.[14]

> John Smith of Walden m. Agnes Charnock of Lancashire
> |
> John – **Thomas** – George – Agnes – Margery – Alice – Jane

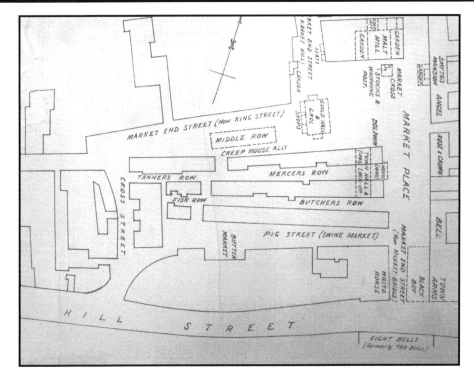

Fig. 5. Walden's market place c.1600s. Smith's family had a house near the north-east corner of the market square and were also linked with the Priory (below).

Fig. 6. The Priory on Common Hill, drawn in the 19th century, showing the older north part of the building. Notice on the right the former Tudor gateway still visible today, and likely to have been in use at the time the Smith family is said to have lived here – see detail, Fig. 7 (right).

There is a further divergence between Dewar and Strype over Smith's education. Strype states that Thomas was educated at the Old School in Walden, meaning the Saffron Walden Free Grammar School; but Dewar says that early traditions associating him with the School are unfounded (Fig. 8).[15] However the Grammar School would be the obvious school for a boy of Smith's ability to attend. The Grammar School can be traced back to 1317 when its existence is mentioned in manuscripts as under one Reginald, 'Scholemaster of Walden'. From that date there are further records of succeeding 'scholemasters'. Education was regarded as the prerogative of the monastic orders, so the school required a licence from the Abbot and Convent of Walden, which it obtained in 1483. In 1522 Dame Johane Bradbury, widow of a former Lord Mayor of London and sister of John Leche, Vicar of Saffron Walden from 1489 to 1521, re-established the old school by letters patent from King Henry VIII. The school curriculum was to be 'after the ordre and use of teaching gramer in the scholes of Wynchester and Eton'.[16] William Cawson or Dawson, who had distinguished himself in singing Mass, and in teaching in the school, was appointed when it became a free school to teach grammar freely to children born in Walden, Little Chesterford, Newport and Widdington, and the children and kinsfolk of Dame Johane. This same William appointed in 1525 may possibly have taught Smith for a short time before he went to Cambridge.

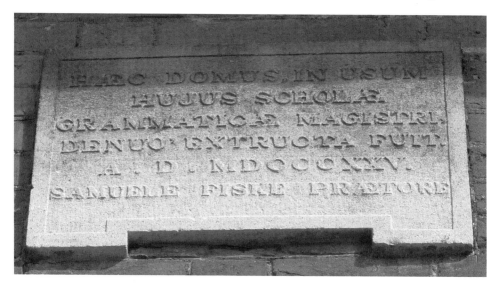

Fig. 8. Plaque on side of house in Castle Street, once the site of the Grammar School.

In 1549 a new charter of incorporation for the school was obtained by Smith, by then Secretary of State, and thus the school became one of the 18 King Edward VI grammar schools in the country. The School was granted a corn-mill and a malt mill near the town and an annuity of £12 pa. Thomas Smith's influence is to be seen in a requirement that the choice of schoolmasters was put in the hands of the President and Fellows of Queens' College, Cambridge, where Smith had been a Fellow and its Vice-President. In August 1549, John Smith and William Strachey are said to have bought lands in and near Walden worth £550, and John Smith acquired a coat of arms. All this suggests that the Smith family was certainly prominent in the life of the town and by now quite prosperous.

Smith wrote an account of his life in Latin. He mentions no school but describes nearly dying from a mysterious illness when aged four. He writes of his childhood and early adolescence as a period of ill health and low spirits. He comes over as a loner, never happier than when reading a book on his own. In his Latin autobiography Smith gives us a brief summary of his childhood:

> In the first and second years of my life, I was lively, playful and prattling, admired above other infants, esteemed a child of the greatest promise, and especially the delight of my father; but when my third year was completed, or thereabouts, after a nightmare in my sleep, I fell into an exceeding great fever, which held me for two or three years, with little hope of life, and from the effects of which I never seemed perfectly relieved until I was twenty-one or twenty-two. During all that time I was low-spirited, seldom laughing, never playing, yet strongly addicted to reading history, to painting, to writing, and even carving; and throughout the same period, almost up to my twenty-fourth year, I was full of eruptions, pimples and sores, with tooth-ache, and continual weak health; yet in literature and the knowledge of languages I was more learned than my masters were able to teach me. In the tenth and eleventh years of my age I had somewhat better health and therefore before the end of my eleventh year, about the feast of Michaelmas 1525, I was sent to the university of Cambridge.[17]

So at the age of 11, Thomas Smith was sent away to Cambridge to continue his education. It is not known who took care of the young boy, but Smith does mention his tutor as a Dr Taylor, a fellow of Queens' College. Two years later in 1527 Smith entered Queens' College, Cambridge as an undergraduate.

2
The Cambridge Scholar

'The Flower of the University'

Fig. 9. The Old Library, Queens' College, Cambridge.

Cambridge

Winds of change were blowing through the university on the Cam when Smith entered Queens' in 1527 (Fig. 9). Lady Margaret Beaufort, Henry VII's mother, had founded Christ's College in 1505 and St John's in 1511. These colleges put themselves in the vanguard of the new 'humanist' learning, which challenged the old tradition-bound scholasticism. Erasmus, the great humanist scholar, had observed ten years earlier, 'Cambridge is a changed place'. Erasmus who had come to the university in 1511 made an immediate impact upon the theology curriculum by teaching ancient Greek, which threatened the supremacy of the Vulgate, the Latin translation of the Bible. In the new climate of learning, Lutheranism quickly spread in Cambridge. The *White Horse Inn*, situated between King's College and St Catherine's, became the hothouse of theological debate. Amongst those who entered the debate were the early Cambridge reformers and Protestant martyrs, Thomas Cranmer (1489-1556 – later Archbishop of Canterbury), Hugh Latimer (1487-1555 – later Bishop of Worcester), Thomas Bilney (1495-1531), Robert Barnes (1495-1540) and others who had met at the *White Horse Inn* to discuss Lutheranism and the new religious ideas coming out of Germany.

Queens' College

Queens' College Cambridge was founded in 1448 by Margaret of Anjou, the wife of Henry VI, and refounded in 1465 by Elizabeth Woodville, the wife of Edward IV. The College was favourable to the Reformation, and to the writings of Erasmus and Luther. Thomas Farman, President 1525-27, hid Luther's books when search was made for them. Simon Heynes, who was President from 1529-1537, assisted in the compilation of the English Communion service.

Fig. 10. John Cheke.

Smith was fortunate in his contemporaries at Cambridge. At Queens' he made friends with John Ponet (1514-56), who was to become Bishop of Worcester. He and Ponet were sympathetic to the new thinking which was to make Cambridge a beacon for Protestantism. At St John's College he made the acquaintance of John Cheke (1514-57 – see Fig. 10) and Roger Ascham (1515-68), both scholars who were to be influential at court. Cheke became the first Regius Professor of Greek and a tutor to the future Edward VI. Ascham acted as Princess Elizabeth's tutor in Greek and Latin between 1548–50, and served in the administrations of Edward VI, Mary 1 and Elizabeth 1. The influence of these reformers persisted at Cambridge. Unlike many of his friends Smith survived to see the establishment of Protestantism under Queen Elizabeth.

Fig. 11. Sir William Butts

Smith studied diligently and despite ill health took his BA in 1530 and was admitted to a fellowship at Queens' when only 18 years of age. However his health and personal circumstances did not improve and he was in a state of near destitution when Sir William Butts, fellow of Gonville College and physician to the King, came to his rescue (Fig. 11). Butts was a known Protestant and associate of Thomas Cranmer.

I was little more than a boy and had no hope of friends, I was desperate from poverty and helplessness and had already meditated abandoning the university and letters when, on account of a report he [Butts} had heard of a disputation of mine in the schools, he summoned me to him, quite untrained and unpolished as I was, entirely unknown to him, and … bade me not to despair, and like a father rather than a patron and friend from that day gave me every hope and encouragement.[1]

Butts not only helped the young Smith financially but also recommended Smith and John Cheke to the King to be appointed King's Scholars. This gave both men a measure of financial independence as well as enhancing their reputation within the University. Cheke said that he and Smith were bound together in love as brothers. The classics were their inspiration and passion, and together they read from the works of the classical masters, such as Plato, Demosthenes, Aristotle and Cicero.

Smith now began a period of steady advancement in his University career. He lectured in natural philosophy and was appointed public orator in 1533. Richard Eden the geographer, whom Smith had tutored privately, described Smith as 'a man of singular learning in all sciences' and the 'flower of the University of Cambridge'.[2] Ascham wrote later that all the younger generation would be ever in Smith's debt for his learning, diligence and fine example. Walter Haddon (1515-72), the Cambridge humanist and reformer, was one like Smith, who introduced Erasmian humanism into English public life. Haddon said that Smith had infused life into every branch of learning at the University and that like St Paul he had been 'all things to all men': 'When Smith is named, we speak not of a man, but as it were the true embodiment of all humanity and the arts.'[3] Smith thrived in academia. He excelled as a teacher, and in his writing was pedantic in his search for the correct word and the precise phraseology. Richard Crewe wrote a *Treatise on the English Language* in 1595 in which he compared Smith to Plato for his mastery of style and grace of language.

Smith became Vice-President of Queens', taking an active part in college life, and showing interest in particular in the garden and the dining hall. Towards the end of his life in 1573 Smith established two scholarships and two fellowships at Queens'. For this he gave Queens' £12.7s.4d as a perpetual rent charge out of the Manor of Oveston. This included £4.7s.4d for his own relatives or the scholars from Walden School, who were to be given priority. He laid down that the lectureships in arithmetic and geometry were not to be read 'as of a preacher out of a pulpit', but with illustrations on paper or 'with a stick or compass in sand or dust to make demonstration that the scholars may both understand the reader and also do it themselves and so profit'.[4]

Fig. 12. Page annotated by Smith from his copy of De Rebus Gestis Francorum by Paulus Aemilius Veronensis. Queens' College Cambridge Library; above, one of Smith's marginal drawings in this book.

In his will Smith donated all his library of 350 books to the College. There are still stored in Queens' Old Library some 90 of these books, of which 64 have been positively identified as part of Smith's bequest. Many of these books bear Thomas Smith's signature in the frontispiece. Smith's library reflected his wide range of interests including law, history, theology, astronomy, architecture, and medicine. They were in Hebrew, French and Italian, as well as in Latin, Greek and English. The Queens' collection includes books by theologians such as Ambrose, Osiander, and Eusebius; by historians such as Tacitus, Bonfinius, Lazius and Cromerus; by classical writers such as Aesop and his fables, Euclid on mathematics, Aetius on medicine, Dioscorides on herbal medicines; and then jurists such as Alciatus, Connanus, Tiraquellus, and Conrad Lagus. There is Agricola on mining and chemistry, Ruellius on plants, Rondeletius on fish, and Paracelsus on surgery. The Bible and the Koran are amongst the collection as are Justinian's Pandects and Gratian's canon law, and the works of Avicenna, the medieval Persian physician and polymath.

One of the most interesting surviving books is *De Rebus Gestis Francorum* by Paulus Aemilius Veronensis (1455-1529), the Italian historian. Aemilius was commissioned to write the history of the kings of France, a work that he left unfinished. Smith has made extensive annotations in this book, as he did in a number of books. But in this case Smith has also left some lively cartoon figures of contemporary characters that he has sketched in the margins (Fig.12). The figures included Henry VIII, Andrea Doria, Suleiman, and Cesare Borgia and other celebrities of the day. The manuscripts in the Queens' library include Sir Thomas Smith's notebook entitled *Recognisances and Examinacions*, and a lot of information on the currency, the plague, medicines and culinary matters. Smith also left money for an annual feast in his memory, one sign that there was a lighter and most generous side to his nature. Queens' still continues to have an annual Thomas Smith feast for the fellows every December.

Regius Professor

Fig. 13 Bishop Stephen Gardiner.

In 1540 King Henry VIII created five Regius Professorships at Cambridge in Divinity, Civil Law, Physic, Hebrew and Greek. These professorships were well-paid at a salary of £40 per annum and hence much coveted. Thomas Smith was created Regius Professor of Civil Law, and his friend John Cheke became Regius Professor of Greek. Smith and Cheke collaborated to try and introduce a new pronunciation of Greek based on single letters representing single sounds. This met with opposition from conservative elements within the University, most notably from Stephen Gardiner, the Chancellor of the University (Fig. 13). Smith responded to Gardiner by producing a work entitled *De Recta et Emendata Linguae Graecae Pronuntiatione*. In the book a character called Quintus persuades Obstinatus of the need for phonetic spelling and the need for a new alphabet since the Latin alphabet did not provide for all the sounds of the English language. It was circulated in manuscript and shown to Gardiner but not published until 1568. Whatever the merits of Smith's pronunciation it did not win favour on the Continent and, faced with the hostility of the Chancellor, Smith backed down. Cheke nonetheless persisted with the campaign, which did not please Gardiner. The new pronunciation was however eventually to win out, and form the basis of Greek as taught in English schools to the end of the 19th century.

Later Smith was to turn his attention to the English language. In the middle 1560s he published a book, *De Recta et Emendata Linguae Anglicae Scriptione Dialogus*. In this book he suggested a new alphabet consisting of 19 Roman/Latin, four Greek and six English letters with ten vowels carrying long or short accents. He proposed the abolition of diphthongs and double consonants. He also wanted to get rid of Q and C, and replace them by KU and K or S respectively. This book has proved useful to scholars seeking to discover the received pronunciation of English words at the time of Shakespeare.

Smith's appointment as Regius Professor of Civil Law was controversial as he was thought by some to be insufficiently qualified in his subject. Smith himself felt daunted by his new post. To increase his knowledge and confidence he took himself off to the Continent to study at the leading law schools. He visited Paris and Orleans and then Padua, where he took a degree in law. On his return to Cambridge Smith delivered his inaugural lectureship and was awarded with two doctorates in law (LlD and DCL). In his inaugural address Smith told his audience that law should be combined with the humanities. The best lawyers possessed the knowledge of physicians, philosophers, orators and poets. Above all law was the subject of moral philosophy not logic. Ethics and law were like twin sisters.[5] He became learned in Civil Law. He was said to be able to cite 600 passages from the Pandects (530-533 AD), a compendium or digest of Roman law compiled by order of the Emperor Justinian.

He earned a reputation as an excellent orator and stylist. 'Had you been there you would have heard another Socrates', wrote Haddon to Cox of one of Smith's university speeches on a formal occasion. Smith appears to have concentrated more on university administration than on Civil Law, and he was rewarded for his efforts by becoming Vice Chancellor in 1543 at the youthful age of 30 years. The son of Saffron Walden was greatly proud of this achievement and confided in his diary: 'I fancied myself supremely happy to have command as it were of the University and that province' of Ely, where he was Chancellor of the Diocese.[6]

Vice-Chancellor

In his capacity as Vice-Chancellor, Smith was involved in the acquisition of a dissolved Carmelite monastery in Cambridge and in a property dispute with the House of Blackfriars, Ludgate. He oversaw a statute which for the first time required all members of the University to be registered and matriculated. But perhaps the greatest service that he rendered to Cambridge was to spare the University from royal expropriation. In 1546 the King demanded that all colleges send in a return of income and expenditure. This was thought to be a prelude to a royal takeover such as had happened to the monasteries. The University looked to the Vice-Chancellor for its salvation and Smith presented a formal petition to the King to spare it. This was done with such diplomacy and skill that both the

King and Catherine Parr praised the letters from the Vice Chancellor, 'Dr Smith your discreet and learned advocate', and assured the University that it was not the royal wish 'to confound those ancient and godly institutions'.[7]

Smith lived carefully but comfortably at Cambridge. He had three servants and three guns, and claimed to keep 'three summer nags and three winter geldings' in his stables. Whilst still at Cambridge in addition to his university appointments Smith was made Chancellor to the Bishop of Ely, which brought in £50 pa, and was collated to the benefice of Leverington, in the Fens near Wisbech, which was worth £36 pa. The Bishop of Ely (Thomas Goodrich) also ordained Smith priest whilst still unmarried in his thirty-third year.

Later when summoned to court it would appear that Smith 'doffed his clerical dress' and resumed life as a layman.[8] The issue as to whether Smith was ordained was to prove contentious in his subsequent appointment as Provost of Eton (Fig. 14). All the time Smith was accumulating the wealth with which he was later able to live the life of a country gentleman at his large mansion Hill Hall.

Fig. 14. Nineteenth-century drawing of Smith, said to be in his 30s, around the time at Cambridge when he fathered an illegitimate child.

During his Cambridge days Smith mentions in his Memoirs that an illegitimate son was born to him: 'Tho Smithus junior 15 March 1547 at 17.20 hours'. In his customary way Smith drew an astrological table based on the precise date and time of the birth. But the entry goes further in giving the exact time and date of conception. 'Conceptus 6 June 1546 at 9.30 hours.'[9] (Fig. 15) The son bears his father's name, but despite giving a time reference for the conception, the mother's identity is not revealed. Much was expected of this only son, hopes and dreams which were not realised. Thomas Smith junior was later to play a large part in Smith's ventures in Ireland.

Even after leaving Cambridge and becoming involved in national affairs, Smith retained an active interest in his alma mater. He came forward with two ambitious proposals. The first was a plan for a college of civil law to be known as 'Edward College', with a master, reader, sublector, examiner and 23 fellows. The Regius Professorship of Civil Law was to be attached to Edward College, to be formed by the merger of Clare College and Trinity Hall. It is not surprising that the proposal aroused great opposition from both these colleges. The House of Commons also intervened to reject the proposed merger. It was suggested that the Regius Professor was getting above himself. Smith's second proposal was for the formation of a College of Civilians (civil lawyers) with a president and twelve fellows to attend upon the Privy Council, the Lord Chancellor and other affairs of the King. This was essentially a plan for a proper civil service of qualified lawyers. This too came to nothing.

Henry VIII died on the 28 January 1547. Shortly afterwards in February 1547, some 20 years after entering the University, Smith left Cambridge to enter the service of Edward Seymour, Earl of Hertford. Seymour was shortly to become the 1st Duke of Somerset and Protector of England. Smith was being pulled into the vortex of political power. His ambition had outgrown Cambridge and the bright light of the court was drawing him upwards.

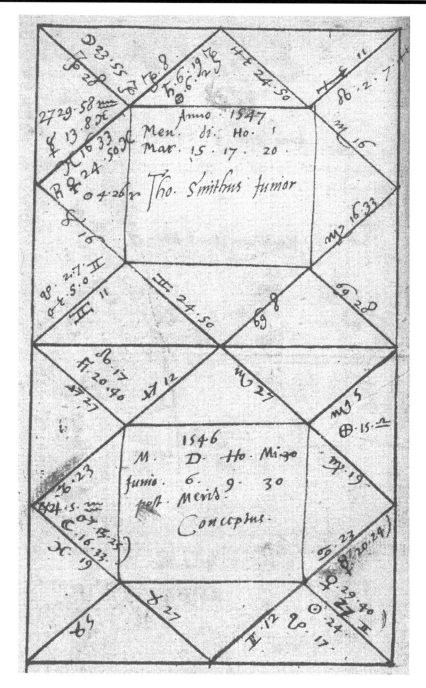

Fig. 15. Smith's astrological table relating to the conception and birth of his illegitimate son. By this it can be seen that Thomas Smith junior was conceived at 9.30 a.m. on 6 June 1546, and born nine months later at 5.20 p.m. on 15 March 1547. The identity of the mother is not known. Interestingly, Smith uses the 24-hour clock on his records.

3
The Edwardian Secretary of State

'The Miserable State of our Commonwealth'

Fig. 16. The boy king, Edward VI.

Edward VI was the son of Henry VIII and his third wife, Jane Seymour, and was born on the 12 October 1537 at Hampton Court Palace (Fig. 16). His mother died twelve days later from postnatal complications. Edward was educated under the care of Richard Cox and John Cheke, whose teaching concentrated on languages, scripture, philosophy and 'all liberal sciences'. Roger Ascham and Jean Belmain assisted in his studies of French, Spanish and Italian, and he learnt to play the lute and the virginals. He was a diligent student and was keen to compete with his sister Elizabeth's academic prowess. He showed a keen interest in reformed theology, and in 1549 wrote a treatise on the Pope as Antichrist. The reign of Edward VI was to see England plainly set on a Protestant course. Clerical celibacy and the mass were abolished and worship became based on Cranmer's Book of Common Prayer. But inflation and the enclosures of common land combined with religious discontent meant that the kingdom remained in a volatile and unsettled condition.

Protector Somerset

Fig. 17. Edward Seymour, Duke of Somerset and Protector.

When Edward VI ascended the throne on the death of his father, Henry VIII, Edward was only nine years and four months of age. In his will Henry had directed that rule should be exercised by a Regency Council. There was no provision for a Protector. But within a matter of days the Privy Council appointed Edward Seymour, 1st Earl of Hertford, as Lord Protector of the Realm and Governor of the King's Person (Fig. 17). Seymour was the older brother of Queen Jane Seymour, the deceased mother of Edward VI, and thus Edward's uncle. In March 1547 Seymour obtained letters patent from the King allowing him to make his own appointments to the Privy Council. He gave himself virtually dictatorial powers to rule by proclamation. At the same time Seymour appointed himself the 1st Duke of Somerset. Seymour's party in the Council were clearly well prepared to take over rule once Henry died. The two most Catholic and conservative members of the Council, Stephen Gardiner and Thomas Howard, Duke of Norfolk, had been sidelined. Norfolk spent Edward's reign in the Tower, his lands having been forfeited and available for distribution to loyalist supporters of the Protector. The appropriation of church property and the minority of the King meant that there were rich spoils to be won by those with sufficient ruthlessness and ambition.

Fig. 18. Sir William Cecil, Lord Burleigh.

So it came about that Smith, attracted as a moth to the light, left the dreamy spires of academia to be catapulted into the cockpit of power politics. It was a trajectory that he sometimes regretted, but it undoubtedly ensured his own personal advancement and prosperity. Smith's advocacy for Cambridge University had brought him to the attention of prominent people in court circles. Furthermore the young King's tutors, John Cheke and Roger Ascham, were Smith's close friends. Somerset was keen to recruit men of learning and ability to join his staff. William Cecil (1521-1598), a graduate of St John's Cambridge and a pupil of Cheke and Ascham, became Somerset's personal secretary (Fig. 18). Smith was appointed Clerk of the Privy Council. This was a prestigious appointment giving him access to the most powerful men in the Kingdom. It carried a yearly salary of £40, which was augmented by the fees collected by the clerks from those having business with the Council. Smith being an 'excellent metallist and chemist' was also appointed Steward of the Stannaries. In addition he was made Master of the Court of Requests.

The Court of Requests was created as part of the Privy Council in order that complaints and cases brought to the Council by the poor should be expedited. It first became an independent tribunal with some Privy Council elements under Henry VII, with jurisdiction mainly over matters of equity. The Court became increasingly popular because it was cheap and speedy in contrast with the slow and expensive common law courts. This aroused the opposition and envy of common law lawyers and judges. Somerset used the Court to extend his power and influence. The hostility that this engendered washed over onto Smith himself.

Somerset's main qualities were as a soldier, which he had already proved in Scotland and in France. Somerset as Lord Protector marched north against the Scots. His prime purpose was to force the marriage of Mary Stuart, the infant Queen of the Scots, to Edward VI. Somerset aimed to unite the two kingdoms and to undermine the corrosive influence of France north of the Tweed. Smith trailed north in Somerset's train. He does not seem to have taken well to travel and lay sick with a fever in York whilst the action took place in Scotland. Somerset won a victory over the Scots at the Battle of Pinkie Cleugh in September 1547, and set up a chain of garrisons in Scotland as far north as Dundee. However the Scots under Mary of Guise, the Queen Regent, were not defeated. Mary, Queen of Scots, was removed to France, where she was betrothed to the French Dauphin. The French sent reinforcements and Edinburgh was saved from the English. The cost of the war and maintaining the garrisons placed an unsustainable burden on the English exchequer. The French attack on Boulogne in August 1549 finally forced Somerset to withdraw from Scotland.

Meantime Smith continued to advance in power and wealth. He became Member of Parliament for Marlborough, and in December 1547 was elected Provost of Eton, which carried a salary of £50 pa, and allowances worth £200. The King had written to the fellows of Eton requesting them to appoint Smith even though he was not ordained as a priest. Later, when under Elizabeth the issue of Smith's ordination was raised, the fellows responded by stating that Smith had preached and taken minor orders, 'benet and colet', at Cambridge.[1] Other preferments came Smith's way. In January 1548 he was made Dean of Carlisle, an appointment which did not require ordination. However the post was not as lucrative as it might have been since the payment of a pension to Smith's predecessor was required to come out of his stipend.

The secret of wealth accumulation in Tudor times lay in the acquisition of land. Smith set about gradually extending his estates. John Thynne, the steward to the Duke of Somerset, set the gold standard for lining one's own pocket. Thynne, whose descendants became the Marquesses of Bath, built Longleat with the proceeds of his stewardship. In October 1547 Smith bought the reversion of the manor of Yarlington, near Wincanton in Somerset, from the Marquess of Northampton. For an outlay of £300, thought to be well below its value, Smith acquired an income of £30 pa, and the profits of the annual fair at Yarlington, as well as the advowson of the rectory. Eyebrows were raised at this sale as Smith had sat on a commission which declared that Northampton's marriage was valid.[2] In April 1549 Smith made a large purchase of lands from the Collegiate Church of All Saints, Derby, which had been recently dissolved. The annual value of the collegiate church was estimated in the 1530s as £38.14s, apart from the considerable share held by the Dean of Lincoln. The sale price was £346.13s.4d. It was purchased by Smith in partnership with his friend, Henry Newsam or Needham. Later Smith bought his partner's share.

Secretary of State

The duties of Clerk to the Privy Council required Smith's regular attendance at court in London. In 1548 he purchased the lease of a house in Canon Row, close by Westminster Bridge, for some 200 marks. But Smith's predilection for economy soon showed itself, for he let his house to William Paget, then Chancellor of the Duchy of Lancaster, and moved in with his brother, George, the London draper. George had a house in Philpot Lane near London Bridge in the City. (Later during the reign of Queen Elizabeth Smith moved back into the Canon Row house.) About the same time, Smith was promoted to Second Secretary of State. His duties were to attend the Privy Council and meetings of Parliament. He drafted Council letters and discussed with the Lord Protector all despatches from ambassadors. Audiences with the Protector or the King would be on a twice daily basis. The annual pay of a Secretary was £200 with 'their table in the court furnished with a mess of meat'. The monthly income from fees could run as high as £400 to £500.

His rise up the career ladder raised questions as to why he was not married. Smith found a young bride in Elizabeth Carkeke, aged 19 years, the daughter of a city printer. Elizabeth's sister was married to Thomas Chamberlain, the Governor of the English community in Antwerp. Smith and Elizabeth were married on 15 April 1548. Elizabeth brought to the marriage a dowry of 1,000 marks, a substantial sum, which Smith used to finance some of his property deals. Elizabeth seems to have been a plain, home-loving girl, little used to the fashionable ways of court. Strype says:

Smith's Lady was a little woman, and one that affected not fine, gaudy cloths, for which she was taxed by some. And by this, one might judge her to have been a woman of prudence and religion, and that affected retirement rather than the splendour of a court. For Dr Smith allowed her what she pleased: and she was his cash-keeper. However, he used to wear goodly apparel, and went like a courtier himself.[3]

Elizabeth incurred the displeasure of the formidable Anne Seymour, Duchess of Somerset, well known for her pride and lofty pretensions. Anne criticised Elizabeth for her dowdy and 'uncourtlike' clothes, and her failure to maintain the standards of hospitality expected of a Secretary's wife. Smith replied, 'She hath all my money; I never debarrid her of peny, and I have often spoken to her, whie she doth not goo more courtlike.'[4] Elizabeth died childless four years later.

Meanwhile Smith was busy with the routine work of the Secretaryship. This included the examination of suspicious characters, especially those accused of 'conjuring' or 'prophesying', for such characters could unsettle people of weak minds. Thus Smith found himself looking into the case of William Wycherley, an alleged sorcerer, who was hired to find a lost silver plate belonging to the household of the Lord Protector. The faint-hearted Wycherley confessed that he was more comfortable using a crystal than in summoning demons.[5] Smith was also involved in more pedestrian tasks, such as the raising and paying of mercenary forces recruited overseas to fight for the King. Munitions, such as guns, saltpetre and other war supplies had to be obtained, principally from the Netherlands. The governing role of the Council and ongoing communications with ambassadors went on week by week.

In 1548 Smith was sent on an embassy to Antwerp to try and deny the ports of the Low Countries to the French, who were in league with the Scots. He also enquired into the grievances of English merchants, whose exclusive control of the export trade in cloth had been withdrawn. Smith succeeded in getting the merchants' privileges restored. But Smith found it necessary to recommend that his brother-in-law, Thomas Chamberlain, should resign as Governor of the English merchants. He failed, however, in his desire to move the staple market for the trade from Antwerp to England. He also negotiated with the Emperor to try and raise a mercenary force of 2,000 soldiers.

Religion

In the Tudor period religion was inextricably intermeshed with politics. People could not conceive how anybody who held heterodox views on religion could be anything but a subversive threatening the established order. Thus as Secretary, Smith dealt not only with what we would regard as secular matters of diplomacy and trade but also with religious questions. Throughout 1548 Smith was actively involved with Archbishop Cranmer and others on the production of a new Prayer Book (Fig. 19). Dewar accuses Smith of bending 'with a detached alacrity to whichever religious wind blew the hardest'.[6] This charge has some force because Smith recognised that survival in public office depended on a keen awareness of current theological trends. For Smith had to learn to live with a country lurching within one generation from Henrician Catholicism to Edwardian Protestantism to Marian repression to Elizabeth's Anglican settlement. Protestants accused Smith of lukewarmness. Catholics accused him of fanaticism. It was said that Smith attacked the catholic doctrine of the eucharist 'with a coarseness of expression which was deliberately offensive'.[7] Probably the truth lies between the two extremes. Smith knew when to keep his head down, but for all that there can be no doubt that he subscribed to a reformed view of Christianity. He certainly made it clear that he had no truck with the Roman doctrine of transubstantiation.

Fig. 19. Archbishop Thomas Cranmer.   *Fig. 20. Bishop Edmund Bonner.*

In 1549 Smith sat on a commission with the Archbishop of Canterbury and four other senior clergy in the examination of heretics, including Anabaptists and Arians, 'that began to spring up apace and show themselves more openly'.[8] Amongst those questioned were the hysteric Joan of Kent, on whom Smith produced a lengthy report in Latin. This was Joan Bocher – not to be confused with other Joans of Kent - who was charged in 1548 with heresy for denying the humanity of Christ in 1548. She was burnt at the stake in 1550.[9] Later in 1549 Smith together with Bishop Ridley of Rochester, Dean May of St Paul's, Sir John Cheke and Dr Wendy, the King's physician, conducted a visitation of the University of Cambridge to abolish such statutes and ordinances as 'maintained papistry, superstition, blindness and ignorance, and to set forth such as might further God's Word and good learning'.

In the summer of 1549 Smith locked horns with Bishop Bonner of London (Fig. 20). Bonner was imprisoned for his opposition to the new ecclesiastical visitation and his questioning of the new political order. Smith told Bonner that, if he wished to redeem himself, he should preach a sermon at St Paul's Cross to state explicitly that the powers of the King were in no way limited by his minority. Bonner's sermon was deliberately equivocal and evasive. Smith examined Bonner who claimed that it was outrageous that he as a bishop should be arrested for disregarding the orders of a mere secretary. Bonner, who was known for his temper, declared that Smith was a 'notorious and manifest enemy', and a thoroughly 'incompetent, unmeet and suspect judge'. Smith told Bonner to make an end of these invented 'oddities and quirks', and ordered his committal to the Marshalsea.[10]

Thomas Seymour was Somerset's highly ambitious younger brother. He was married to Catherine Parr, the widow of Henry VIII. Seymour was given the office of Lord High Admiral, but this sop did not placate him. He made life as difficult as possible for the Lord Protector, and sought to gain influence over Princess Elizabeth and Lady Jane Grey and to build up his own power base at court. A coup d'état was suspected. Sharington, the keeper of the Bristol mint, was accused of coining money illegally to support the plot. Smith conducted lengthy interrogations of the Admiral and Sharington. Seymour was taken to the Tower. In March 1549 Parliament passed a bill of attainder against Seymour and he was executed. His brother the Lord Protector made no attempt to intervene.

Knighthood

Fig. 21. Engraving of Sir Thomas Smith by Houbraken.

That same spring Smith was put in charge of a small team of lawyers and others to establish England's right to sovereignty over Scotland, a key strategy of Somerset. In the autumn Somerset published a document entitled, *An Epitome of the Title that the King's Majesty of England hath to the Sovereignty of Scotland.* Smith appears to have been the principal author of this tract, which contains the bold claim, 'I have studied a great while the laws of this realm and be it said without arrogance have read them all both old and new'.

In April 1549 Smith was knighted (Fig. 21). All was not going smoothly however. He had incurred the enmity of the Duchess of Somerset, and in a letter to her defended himself against accusations of being 'a sore and extreme man ... an oppressour ... a great chopper and chaunger of land'.[11] Furthermore, Bishop Latimer attacked Smith in a sermon: 'For what an enormity this is in a Christian realm, to serve in the civility having the profits of provostship, and a deanery and a parsonage. But I tell you what will become of it, it will bring the clergy into slavery.'[12] The message seems to have got home, for a couple of months later Smith resigned the parsonage at Leverington.

The regime of Somerset's Protectorate was becoming increasingly unpopular. There was a rising in the West Country against the new Prayer Book. Exeter was besieged for over a month. German mercenaries had to be called in to suppress the uprising, which left 4,000 rebels dead. There were serious economic problems and widespread unrest in the country. In June 1548 Somerset was forced to set up a commission to look into enclosures in the Midlands, which were causing disturbances amongst the dispossessed peasantry. In Norfolk a serious rebellion broke out over the issue of enclosures and poverty in July 1549. Fifteen thousand rebels under the leadership of Robert Kett of Wymondham captured the city of Norwich. Eventually the rebels were crushed by troops under the command of John Dudley, Earl of Warwick. But the disturbances were by no means restricted to Norwich. There were local uprisings in Norfolk, Suffolk, Essex. Kent and elsewhere.[13] They reflected the emergence of a formerly repressed class of working people who were no longer content to suffer silently and passively. This was precisely the danger to the social fabric which conservatives had warned would be the consequence of allowing the libertarian ideas of the New Testament to foment popular discontent.

Prices soared during the 16th century, rising by 50 per cent between 1500 and 1540, and more than doubling over the next 20 years. The price of wheat rose fourfold in 1549 causing considerable hardship. The economic situation was worse, compounded by a debased coinage and widespread counterfeiting, which led to inflation and discontent. On 22 June 1549 Smith reported to Somerset on the financial situation. His recommendations for reform were ignored by Somerset, who was personally profiting from the debased coinage to the extent, it was alleged, of making nine shillings for every pound of coin minted. Smith later wrote:

The abating of the standard is a manifest token of the decay of the state and a continual undoing unto it, for as the money abases so do all things enhance. Now of late when the coin was so excessively altered and so manifestly made lighter and worse … not only wages but also all things upon it did start up to those excessive prices which we have seen.[14]

A Discourse of the Commonweal of England

Fig. 22. Title page from Sir Thomas Smith's The Commonwealth of England published in 1581.

Smith was disgusted at the response of the Lord Protector and took himself off to Eton where he stayed for the next three months. He wrote to Cecil: 'I have of long time, as methinks marvellous long time, lamented the miserable state of our commonwealth.'[15] Smith was not idle at Eton. He had time to reflect on the dire economic situation in a treatise entitled, *A Discourse of the Commonweal of England* (Fig 22). This book has been hailed by the economist Murray Rothbard as the first account of mercantalist doctrine by an English writer.[16] Mercantalism, which later morphed into protectionism, was based on government control of foreign trade as an instrument of a state's political and economic policy. Mercantalism was to dominate European thinking from the 16th to the late 18th centuries. The book took the form, which Smith often employed, of a dialogue between different characters, in this case a doctor (who expressed the author's own views) a knight, a merchant, a farmer and other characters. They discussed the relationship between a debased coinage, inflation, high prices and social disintegration. He makes mention of the disturbances in the country in the summer of 1549 when, as Strype put it, the people 'brake out partly for enclosures, and partly for religion into an open and formidable insurrection in most counties of England'.[17] The work was in manuscript, and not published until 1581, but was for Cecil's attention.[18] Somerset, whose war policy was financed by debasement, remained deaf to the economic arguments. Smith also argued against the moralists that man's acquisitiveness could be channelled towards the common good, using covetousness and greed as an unavoidable part of the human condition.

William Paget, perhaps Somerset's closest adviser, wrote the Lord Protector a blunt letter in which he urged strong action and laid the blame for the social unrest on the head of Somerset, 'your own laxity, your softness, your opinion to be good to the poor'. Somerset was seen to be ambivalent on enclosures. His appointment of commissioners to investigate enclosures in the midland counties, suggested that he was sympathetic to the people's grievances, but put him out of favour with the landlords. When Smith returned to court in September 1549 he felt it necessary to defend his own conduct. In his letter to the Duchess of Somerset, Smith denied the charge of religious lukewarmness, of being oppressive in his judgements and of personal covetousness. He claimed that he had dismissed two servants when bribery was alleged in the Court of Requests. His prosperity, he said, was due to the wise and prudent investments of his brother, George, in the City. The Canon Row House was not really his, but George's. As to his manners, he said that he was impatient with trivialities. He liked to think of himself as a straightforward man who spoke his own mind.[19]

The Rise of Warwick

Smith's return to court coincided with an attempt by members of the Council led by John Dudley, Earl of Warwick, to get rid of Somerset. Somerset, together with several hundred of his own men, took himself to the King at Hampton Court Palace and called on all loyal citizens to defend the King and the Protector. On 5 October 1549 he issued a proclamation accusing 'traitors and murderers' of preventing him from calling Parliament. He was contemptuous of his opponents, whom he referred to as men 'come up of late from the dunghill: a sort of them more meet to keep swine than the offices which they do occupy … a monstrous Council'.[20]

Smith and Sir William Petre, the two Secretaries of State, sent urgent appeals to Russell and Herbert in the West Country to bring their troops to Somerset's aid. They turned a deaf ear. Petre was sent to London to negotiate with Warwick. He did not return. Smith remained loyal to the Lord Protector and moved with Somerset and the King to Windsor. Cranmer and Smith urged Somerset to avoid a bloody confrontation. Warwick and the lords with him demanded that Somerset lay down his arms for 'we be almost the whole Council'. A reply was drafted and signed by Cranmer, Paget and Smith in which they stated that Somerset offered to give up the Protectorship, but that 'to put himself simply into your hands is not reasonable … Life is sweet my Lords and they say you seek his blood and his death'.[21]

On 9 October word was received from Russell and Herbert to the effect that they would support Warwick rather than Somerset. George Smith brought word to Smith of the Lords' proclamation, which referred to 'the malice and evil government of Edward, Duke of Somerset, lately called Protector', and detailed his abuses. An open letter to the King was read in the great hall at Windsor. This stated that no harm was intended to Somerset's life, lands or goods, but said that he only held office at the King's pleasure. A private letter to Cranmer, Paget and Smith took them to task and held them answerable for the safety of the King. These men in any event had no wish to fight over the King.

The game was clearly up. On 11 October the Lords sent Wingfield down to Windsor and Somerset was arrested.[22] Two days later the Council sat. Smith, Stanhope, Thynne, Wolf and Gray were all committed to the Tower, along with Somerset. Smith was sequestered from the Council, deprived of his Secretaryship and replaced by Wotton. Smith had climbed to the top of the slippery pole and had come crashing down again. In the Tower, Smith ruminated on his fate and wrote these lines:

> He that is most high is most nere th' assault
> The fortunes of men be so wonderful.
> This day made new Duke, Marquis or Baron
> Yet may the axe stand near the dore.
> Everthing is not ended as it is begone
> God will have the stroke, either after or before.[23]

4
The Wilderness Years

'Utterly Forgotten'

Provost of Eton

Smith used his time in the Tower to reflect on the fickleness of fortune. He translated some of the more mournful psalms into English and composed prayers for deliverance. He wrote a book of poetry of no great quality. He also found comfort in astrology, which he had previously despised. After four months' incarceration Smith was released along with others, upon a recognizance of £3,000 and a requirement to be 'from day to day forthcoming'.

Smith fled London and retired to the comparatively quiet life of Provost of Eton College. His personal wealth remained intact. In the summer of 1550 he paid over £400 in cash and returned property to the Crown as purchase price for the manors of Ankerwicke, Overton and Oveston in Buckinghamshire, Ankerwicke-Pernishe in Surrey and Bynderton in Surrey. The yearly value of these properties was estimated at nearly £90. Smith rebuilt the ruined manor house at Ankerwicke near Eton on land overlooking Runnymede on the opposite side of the river.[1] This was Smith's home for the rest of the reign of Edward VI and for most of Mary's reign. Shortly after taking up residence, Smith acquired the neighbouring property of Wyrardsbury, now known as Wraysbury.

As Provost, Smith kept a close eye on the finances of the college and was strict in the collection of college rents. He entrusted much of the management of the finances to Humphrey Mitchell, who stayed with Smith for twenty years. In 1595 the Queen was informed by a later Provost, Sir Henry Savile, that Smith had been 'the best head and the most beneficial that ever the college had'.[2] Smith introduced a new kind of inflation-proof lease whereby the tenant paid a fixed part of the rent in wheat or malt. Later towards the end of his life he introduced this kind of lease in his Act for the Maintenance of the Universities. The Provost also oversaw some building including a new kitchen and cellar, and new gardens were laid out under his direction. Despite the stipend and allowances which should have amounted to over £200, Smith complained that he was out of pocket at Eton, and that he had had to pay over £100 of his own money to equip the college servants with new liveries. He was canny enough to keep a lot of the college business within his family: his brother George supplied the liveries; the college's legal work was conducted by Smith's cousin, George Nicholls of Walden; and the account books were looked after by John Wood, who was Smith's favourite nephew and secretary. In 1550 Smith accepted 42 pound weight of old college plate in lieu of a shortfall of £120 out of £250 due to the Provost.

In January 1551 Smith found himself thrust back into to the maelstrom of national affairs when he was summoned to give evidence in the trial of Bishop Gardiner for a sermon preached three years earlier which was alleged to be subversive. Smith largely shielded Gardiner by evading hostile questions, and his friendship with Gardiner was to bear fruit during Mary's reign. He also found himself on a commission to punish those who opposed the new Prayer Book. Then in May 1551 Smith was appointed to a commission to conclude a treaty of marriage between Edward VI and Princess Elizabeth, the daughter of King Henry II of France. As a sweetener Henry II was invested with the Order of the Garter. The formal betrothal was completed in the Treaty of Angers, which was sealed on 19 July. Henry II conferred the Order of St Michael on the English King. Smith seems to have been prominent in the negotiations, and his language skills would have proved very useful to the English team. However, the premature death of Edward VI aborted the marriage proposal.

Fig. 23. John Dudley, Duke of Northumberland.

In view of the success of the marriage commission it is strange that Smith received no further employment in the service of the State. He might have expected to have been appointed to one of the various commissions, such as the one studying the reform of ecclesiastical canon law, or that investigating heresy, but nothing came his way. It seems that his closeness to Somerset meant that he was never fully accepted within the political circles around John Dudley, Earl of Warwick and newly created Duke of Northumberland, who as President of the Council was now the prime power in government (Fig. 23). The marriage of Northumberland's son John with Somerset's daughter Anne was intended to bring reconciliation, but the plotting and intrigue continued. In January 1552 Northumberland moved decisively against Somerset and his associates. Somerset was arrested and charged with planning a 'banquet massacre' in which the Council was to be assaulted and Northumberland killed. Somerset was acquitted of treason, but in January 1552 was condemned and executed for the technical felony of raising a contingent of armed men without a licence. These events contributed to Northumberland's growing unpopularity.

Smith's rural idyll at Eton was disturbed throughout 1552 by allegations brought against him by certain of the fellows. It appears that the bone of contention was the appointment by the Provost of William Barker as Master for Life. Barker was an old colleague of Smith, and the fellows objected to him because he was married and regarded as an unsuitable candidate. The Privy Council sent a powerful commission to Eton to investigate the charges. The

commission, which included the Duke of Northumberland, the Marquess of Northampton, the Lord Chamberlain, Mr Secretary Petre and Mr Secretary Cecil, found in favour of Smith. At the conclusion of the proceedings, the commission dined in college with the Provost. The cost of the meal is recorded as £15 2s 7d.

Fig. 24. Lady Jane Grey.

The fifteen-year-old King became seriously ill in February 1553 and died on 6 July that year. The King had been keen to exclude his two half-sisters, Mary and Elizabeth, from the succession, as he feared that Mary would re-introduce Roman Catholicism. In his will he named Lady Jane Grey and her male heirs as his successors (Fig. 24). Lady Jane Grey, the grand-daughter of Henry VII, and Northumberland's daughter-in-law, was proclaimed Queen on 10 July. Meanwhile

Princess Mary, who had assembled an armed following in East Anglia, demanded that the Council recognise her as Queen. On 20 July the Council proclaimed Mary as Queen and commanded Northumberland to disband the Army. Northumberland obeyed and in Cambridge market place proclaimed Mary Tudor as Queen. Northumberland was made the scapegoat. He was tried and condemned in Westminster Hall and beheaded on 22 August, having recanted his Protestant faith.

Smith was safely out of the way at Eton during these momentous events. But he found himself summoned 'to make his undelayed repair to the court'. He was greeted by a mocking Bonner, reinstated as Bishop of London. He might well have found himself re-interned in the Tower, but it would appear that Stephen Gardiner spoke up for him, doubtless recalling how Smith had given favourable testimony when Gardiner himself had been in the dock. Smith was however forced to resign as Dean of Carlisle and as Provost of Eton. Later, he was to be accused of misappropriating poor funds at Carlisle, but he was cleared and his accusers were committed to the Fleet. Smith was compensated by being awarded a pension of £100 per annum for services rendered as Secretary. He had not been receiving, as was his right, his pension since the fall of Somerset. It may be that the renewal of his pension was connected with a *Memorandum for the Understanding of the Exchequer*, which Smith wrote for the benefit of the Council. This memorandum supported the revaluation of foreign coins. It was used by Gardiner, who was trying to raise loans in Antwerp, in a dispute with Sir Thomas Gresham, who objected to the revaluation policy of the Council.

Fig. 25. Hill Hall pictured in 1760. The East Front was altered in the early 18th century, but the picture does give us an idea of how Smith's original house looked.

Elizabeth Carkeke, Smith's wife, died on the very day that Queen Mary made her triumphal entry into London. Within a year, on 23 July 1554, Smith married again. His wife was a wealthy childless widow in her mid-thirties. Philippa, daughter of Henry Wilford, a London merchant, and widow of Sir John Hampden of Essex. Philippa brought wealth into the marriage, in particular the manor of Theydon Mount in Essex. This was to become Smith's main home for the remaining 24 years of his life. The estate included the mansion house of Hill Hall (which he was to substantially rebuild), together with 1,000 acres of arable land, 500 acres of meadows and pastures, and 400 acres of woods and heath (Fig. 25). Smith was also fortunate to find a parliamentary seat as member for Grampound. This was a rotten borough in Cornwall in which the Hampden family seem to have had some kind of interest. Certainly the famous politician John Hampden (*c.*1595-1643) was first elected to Grampound in the Parliament of Charles I.

Smith showed the generous side of his nature by offering hospitality to John Taylor, the Bishop of Lincoln, who had incurred Mary's displeasure. Bishop Taylor was allowed to live at Ankerwicke for eight months until his death in December 1554.

The Shakespearian canon

Fig. 26. Edward de Vere.

At the same time a place in Smith's household was made available for Edward de Vere, the four-year-old son of the Earl of Oxford. Some scholars consider Edward de Vere to be the true author of the Shakespearian canon (Fig. 26). He was brought up in the Reformed faith, and whilst living in Smith's household, he was tutored by Thomas Fowle, a former fellow of St John's College, Cambridge. In November 1558 de Vere matriculated as an *impubes* (or immature fellow-commoner), of Queens', Smith's old college.

Amongst the advocates for Edward de Vere, Earl of Oxford, as the true author of the Shakespearian canon, is an American writer, Stephanie Hopkins Hughes. She argues that Sir Thomas Smith is the real literary tutor and mentor behind Edward de Vere. William of Stratford, she claims, was a provincial family man in need of cash who sold his name to the Lord Chamberlain's men so that their playwright Edward de Vere might retain anonymity and privacy for his plays, which bore the name of Shakespeare.

> During the period of most intense education of the nobility, possibly since Alexander was tutored by Aristotle, the first gush of the burst of energy in fields of scholarship, education, and scientific questioning brought by the English Reformation, a great university scholar and teacher spent eight years tutoring a single student, the overly sheltered little scion of one of the last of a dying race, the medieval English nobility. That tutor was the great Sir Thomas Smith, known to his students as the flower of Cambridge University. That student was Edward de Vere, heir to the Oxford earldom. Apart from the knowledge of ancient Greek and Latin philosophy, history, and literature, that Smith necessarily taught little Edward are five interests, one might call them passions, that lie outside the standard curriculum. That Shakespeare should be so steeped in these five areas is one of the leading arguments for Oxford as Shakespeare. These five areas of interest are the Law, astronomy/astrology, the garden, medicine (or physic), and hawking.[3]

The matter must remain not proven, however intriguing the suggestion that England's finest bard might have a closer connection with Essex than Warwickshire!

Queen Mary

Queen Mary was determined to restore England to the Roman Catholic faith and the authority of the Pope (Fig. 28). After the death of the Lord Chancellor, Bishop Stephen Gardiner, in November 1555, and Mary's failure to produce an heir, the pressure of persecution increased. Nearly 300 people were burnt at the stake. Amongst the Protestant martyrs was Robert Smith, a former servant of Sir Thomas Smith. Thomas Smith was vulnerable but kept his head down. He even managed to get himself named on a papal bill of indulgence obtained by William Smithywick, his fellow MP for Grampound. The indulgence granted pardon for any offences, past, present or future, against the Church of Rome. He was also permitted to receive the sacrament privately, and in Lent to eat meat and dairy products without scruple of conscience. In those uncertain times it acted as a wonderful insurance policy.

Figs. 27, 28. Two Queens of England – Elizabeth I (left) and her half-sister Mary I.

Smith concentrated on improving his mansion and his estate. He described his life as 'having been these many years at home, passing my time now and then with hawking and hunting and now and then looking on a book'.[4] His diaries for 1556-57 record little but thunderstorms, strange astrological events and menacing 'signs'. Later he lamented 'the burning of poor men and women for religion, the marriage with Spain, the loss of Calais, and the reduction of the Kingdom to the lowest ebb both in wealth and reputation that it had been in for some hundreds of years before'.[5] Strype comments:

And so he made a shift to pass through this dangerous reign in safety. Following his studies and contemplations in his native country of Essex at his house of Hill-hall there. And when many on all hands of him were most cruelly burnt alive for the profession of that religion which he held, he escaped and was saved even in the midst of the fire. Which probably he might have an eye to in changing the crest of his coat of arms, which now was a salamander living in the midst of a flame; whereas before it was an eagle, holding a writing Pen, flaming in his dexter claw, as may be seen upon a monument of his ancestors in Walden Church...[6]

Queen Elizabeth

'This is the Lord's doing; it is marvellous in our eyes.' These words from Psalm 118 v. 23 were said to have been Elizabeth's response when she was formally told at Hatfield House that her half-sister Mary had died at St James' Palace on 17 November 1558, and that she, Elizabeth, was now Queen (Fig. 27). Sir Thomas Smith, waiting anxiously at Hill Hall for the latest news, might reasonably have expected to have been summoned to fill some great office of state. But no such summons came, although he was given some particular tasks mainly at the instigation of his friend, William Cecil, who became Elizabeth's Secretary of State and closest adviser. Elizabeth herself seems to have distrusted Smith, possibly because of his close association with the Seymours.[7] Smith's first job was to sit on a commission 'for the consideration of things necessary for a parliament'. He also took his seat as MP for Liverpool, which at that date was just another rotten borough with a population of around 600. There was a quarrel at Queens' College, and Cecil wrote to the College suggesting that Smith should mediate.

In July 1559 Smith was appointed to a commission to look into heresies, seditions and other deviations, which might imperil the new religious settlement. According to Strype, Smith was convenor of a distinguished group of clergy who met at his house in Canon Row to revise Edward's Book of Common Prayer (BCP). He had earlier been involved with Cranmer and the BCP, and it would be fascinating to learn what part Smith played in its actual compilation. The group included Matthew Parker, soon to become Archbishop of Canterbury, and some four future bishops. Later that year Smith found himself on the commission overseeing the taking of oaths by the clergy to the new Acts of Supremacy and Uniformity. Smith worked mainly in the dioceses of Ely and Norwich. He also assisted the young Earl of Oxford in receiving a delegation from the Duke of Friesland, who came to offer the hand of his brother, Eric XIV of Sweden, to Elizabeth. But Smith found himself excluded from commissions on the alteration of religion, and on the debasement of the coinage, where he felt he could bring specialist knowledge. Dudley had tried to debase the currency in 1551 with disastrous results. Smith returned to the attack and wrote a treatise on *The Wages of a Roman Footsoldier*, 1562. He compared Roman and English money, and used the opportunity to condemn debasement of the coinage, which brought losses to all and disaster to the Crown. Debasement, said Smith, was evidence of 'the decay of the state' and as a cause of 'excessive prices'.

For several years Smith raged at home complaining that he was 'utterly forgotten'. After much agitation he managed to obtain the restitution of the deanery at Carlisle. But he found himself involved in a dispute concerning the manor at Ankerwicke, where ownership was claimed by the brothers Edmund and Thomas Windsor. The Windsors with a band of 20 men forcibly occupied Ankerwicke and, with swords and daggers drawn, evicted Smith's household. The Windsors took the keys and maliciously damaged some of the furniture. Smith attempted with his servants to reoccupy the property. This lead to a fight in the night with swords and bows and arrows. Smith appealed to the Star Chamber for redress. His suit was successful and his entitlement was upheld to peaceful occupation of the property. Smith used his extended absence from court to attend to his own lands. He moved to the farmhouse at Mounthall, whilst he embarked on an extensive redevelopment of Hill Hall.

Proposals for the Queen's Marriage

Upset at being sidelined, Smith sought to win the Queen's favour by suggesting a variety of proposals for her marriage. Elizabeth seems to have been put off sexual relations by the abuse suffered at the hands of Thomas Seymour, but she knew better than anybody the importance of producing an heir. Knowing Elizabeth's attraction to Lord Robert Dudley, Master of the Horse, Smith sought to promote his cause. However, he faced strong opposition to this from William Cecil and Nicholas Throckmorton and others. Furthermore the death of Dudley's wife, Amy Robsart, in a mysterious fall down stairs, caused scandal and speculation. In April 1561, Smith produced his 'Dialogue on the Queen's Marriage'. This took the form of a dialogue between four friends discussing the pros and cons of the Queen marrying an English nobleman or a foreign prince. The four are 'Spiteweed' (for virginity), 'Lovealien' (for foreign marriage), 'Agamias' and 'Homefriend' (both arguing for an Englishman as superior to any foreigner). It is not known how the Queen reacted to this far from subtle approach. But a few years later Smith wrote to Dudley:

> I am glad that the Queen took my poor house at Ankerwicke but sorry that my wife was not there at the time to entertain Her Highness… I pray God may once see Her Majesty merry there and your Lordship together. Then I shall reckon my house twice sanctified and blessed.[8]

Dudley, who was created Earl of Leicester in 1564, remained a candidate for the Queen's affections for nearly another decade, and Smith continued to push his cause. In April 1563 Smith boldly wrote to the Queen pouring scorn on the idea that she should marry young Charles IX of France, arguing that he was far too young and she too old and it would be like Mary Tudor marrying Philip of Spain, where 'Men did call her the King's Grandmother'. She should marry Dudley: 'I do not see what should let Your Highness to perform it, nor any subject of yours would repine at it'.[9] Elizabeth was not amused!

In September 1562 Smith's nine long years of waiting for an official appointment came to an end. He was appointed Ambassador to France – a post that was to become something of a poisoned chalice. He was to share the embassy with Nicholas Throckmorton, who would prove a hostile colleague. As Smith put it, 'I am set to fly with clipped wings'. France was verging on civil war and there was deep enmity between Huguenots and Catholics. Furthermore, England had lost Calais to the French in 1558, and Elizabeth wanted it back.

5
The Elizabethan Envoy

'I wax now old and therefore unlusty and desiring of rest'.

Ambassador to France

Smith left for France on 22 September 1562. He presented himself at the French court on 29 October. It was not an auspicious beginning. The Catholic forces under the Duke of Guise had taken Rouen and battle with the Huguenots under the Prince of Condé was imminent. The Huguenots had agreed that the English should occupy Le Havre as a pledge for the surrender of Calais in return for 6,000 men and 140,000 crowns. Smith's colleague, Nicholas Throckmorton, did not bother to meet him (Fig. 29).

Fig. 29. Sir Nicholas Throckmorton.

Throckmorton, who had been brought up in the household of the Parr family, regarded Smith as a parvenu. He taunted him as 'having come to court but yesterday as a beggarly scholar'.[1] The Queen Mother, Catherine de Medici, was distinctly hostile, and Smith found nobody with whom he could negotiate. It seemed that only the papal legate, the Cardinal of Ferrara, could tell Smith what was going on. Smith recommended Elizabeth to press on with her policy of urging reconciliation rather than civil war on the French. Smith's relationship with Throckmorton was a fraught one, not only on personal but also on policy grounds. Throckmorton saw his mission as assisting the Huguenots, whilst Smith's aim was to get Calais restored to English sovereignty.

Everything changed however with the Battle of Dreux on 15 December 1562, when the Huguenots were defeated and Condé was taken prisoner along with Throckmorton. It was largely through the good offices of the Cardinal that Catherine gave Throckmorton safe conduct to leave France. It was galling to Smith that Elizabeth shortly afterwards sent Throckmorton back to be joint ambassador with himself. Popular opinion was hostile to the English cause. Smith's servants were attacked in the street and his house surrounded by hostile crowds. One day, returning from court, Smith only reached home safely because of the Cardinal's assistance. The French Provost ordered Smith to leave the house. Smith found basic lodgings out of Paris with only 'one chamber in which to dine, lie and write', and this cost him £120. He moaned that he would be better off in the Tower. But Admiral Coligny rallied the Huguenot forces in Normandy. At this juncture Smith now demanded the return of Calais and the payment of 200,000 crowns, increased at Elizabeth's insistence to 500,000 crowns. In February 1563 when the Duke of Guise was assassinated, Smith was hopeful that Calais could be regained. Never one to miss a chance, he asked Elizabeth that she 'will not forget me in the distributing of lands and offices about Calais as I was forgotten at Her Majesty first coming to her Crown'.[2]

But Smith was over-optimistic and the cause languished. By May he was missing his 'plough' and 'caves' and urging the Queen to send him back home. A weary truce between Catholics and Huguenots settled into a joint hostility towards the English forces in Le Havre, which was captured by the French in July. Elizabeth was displeased: 'We find no such success as we meant' in our embassy, she said.[3] In August the French declared war. Smith and Throckmorton were arrested. Smith was held under house arrest at Melun and Poissy, and for six weeks was without books or papers until his release in September. Throckmorton remained in prison convinced that Smith did 'marvellously concur' in his confinement. Throckmorton grew angrier, attacking Smith as 'this malicious man with his crafty and lewd dealing' who was throwing the English cause away through ignorance, ineptness and folly. Furthermore, Smith discovered that Throckmorton had completely captured Dudley's ear and that most of the Council and the Queen were against him. But Cecil remained constant, 'being so loving and faithful a friend as you are to stick unto me against all my despisers and backbiters'.[4] Before the signing of the Treaty of Troyes in April 1564 the argument between Smith and Throckmorton came to a head with Throckmorton denouncing Smith as a 'fool' and a 'beggarly knave'. The two men closed on one another with daggers drawn, and had to be restrained by their servants.

The Treaty of Troyes 1564

The Treaty of Troyes brought peace between England and France. Elizabeth gave up her claim to Le Havre in return for the payment of 120,000 crowns. Although under the Treaty of Cateau-Cambrésis (1559), the French had promised to restore Calais or pay a large indemnity, in the 1564 Treaty both sides reserved their claims on Calais, which meant in effect that Calais was lost. Freedom of commerce was agreed. The Order of the Garter was conferred on the French King, Charles IX. Smith played a prominent role in the ceremonies surrounding the signing of the Treaty. He delivered a long address in Latin, which was much admired, and accompanied Lord Hunsdon in the Queen's barge. He was rewarded for his part in the drawing up of the Treaty by a handsome present from the French King of a 'cupboard of gilt plate, weighing 1,154 ozs', which was estimated to be worth between 500 and 600 marks.[5]

Smith might reasonably have hoped that after the successful conclusion of the Treaty of Troyes, he might have been allowed to return home and be found a further appointment. However he was to be disappointed and was to spend a further two more years trailing around behind the French King. The King went on a tour of his provinces in the south and the west. Smith complained, 'The Court was like a running camp and never stable in one place'. He was tired and wanted 'to rest home with my wife like an old doting fool.... Neither my body or my spirit can endure travel. I wax now old [he was now 51] and therefore unlusty and desiring of rest'.[6]

Travels in France

In Lyons in July, Smith found every third house shut with plague, the dead unburied, the streets deserted and food very scarce. The heat exhausted him and he was prone to minor illnesses, toothaches, fevers, agues and general misery. The weather was bad, with heavy rain alternating with extreme heat and sometimes cold. On one occasion he lost half his apparel, three horses and all their saddles and bridles in a fire. On another occasion 'in rain and hail and the weather intolerable', his carts were overthrown and he was stuck in the muddy fields all night without shelter. This was no state for the Queen's representative to find himself in. Furthermore, he was short of money as it proved difficult to get funds from England. He complained that the embassy ruined him financially. He was paid £3 6s 8d a day and expenses. But he claimed that his 20 servants cost him 12d a day each for drink, which would cost him only 2d in England. However, he still managed to enjoy the ambassadorial life, to give regular gifts to the Queen, and to buy his wife some fine bracelets and rings.

In February 1565 Smith and his attendants were caught up in a fight in Burbois. Some 20 or 30 swords were drawn. His cook was set upon and his tailor was 'thrust in the buttocks'. Eventually the assailants were driven off with four or five dangerously hurt and likely to die, and five or six more hurt but not seriously. One of Smith's servants received fatal wounds. It was perhaps no surprise after these happenings that in March 1565 Smith should fall desperately ill near Toulouse with a high fever and total disablement: 'My right eye and cheek and half my upper lip was marvellously swollen as though I had been poisoned, but it began with toothache'.[7] He described in detail the remedies and blood lettings and gave accounts of the thickness and redness of each bowel movement. His recovery he attributed to good food and the precious 'waters' from his stills at Mounthall. His servants were not all so fortunate, and he buried a number of them in France. Cecil grew weary of these hypochondriacal reports and urged Smith to send only good news.

In truth Smith had not a great deal of official business to do. He worked to obtain the release of English prisoners held on French galleys. He reported to Elizabeth that Catherine offered to bestow the Order of St Michael on Dudley. The Queen was furious. She did not approve of any of her subjects wearing an order not held by her, and because it would arouse envy. She was eventually persuaded to agree to Dudley having the Order, provided that it was awarded to Norfolk as well. Smith continued with desultory negotiations about the Queen marrying Charles IX or the Duke of Orleans. He still thought that she should marry Dudley before she got too old. Her refusal seemed to him to be wanton folly in gambling the nation's safety on her life.

Smith used his enforced stay in France to enlarge his mind. He made a study of classical architecture. He was planning the alterations to his large mansion, Hill Hall, and was especially taken with the Chateau de Bournazel near Toulouse. He admired the Roman amphitheatres at Nîmes and Arles, commenting on their 'marvellous magnificence, great art and sumptious buildings both for the space of round and the highness of the stone'.[8] He visited Geneva and appreciated meeting with the biblical scholar Theodore Beza, Calvin's successor as leader of Reformed Protestantism. Smith was interested in plants and sent home to his wife 'certain roots of hyacinths and two or three of asphodel [the flowers of the Elysian fields, according to classical mythology] because I have not seen them before in England'.[9] He conducted learned correspondence with Haddon and political discussions with Cecil for whom he collected books on armoury and genealogy. He had little time for court banquets or jousts or military carnivals. He preferred hunting and hawking. He urged the Queen and Cecil to adopt a new calendar because the Julian calendar was out of step with the seasons by some ten days. Smith was far ahead of his times. The calendar promulgated by Gregory XIII in 1582 was not adopted in Britain until 1752, two hundred years later.

De Republica Anglorum

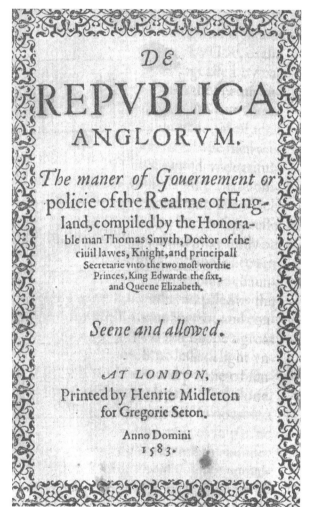

Fig. 30. Title page from De Republica Anglorum 1583 by Thomas Smith, a copy of which is in Saffron Walden Town Library.

Smith's earlier books on English and Greek pronunciation were published in Paris. Between 1562 and 1565 he wrote his major work, *De Republica Anglorum: A Discourse on the Commonwealth of England* (Fig. 30). It was a complete summary of Elizabethan government, the judicial system, Parliamentary powers and procedures. It also presented a classical vision of England based on the models of ancient Greece and Rome. Smith sought to explain how English law differed from Roman law on the Continent. In a memorable passage, he lambastes the corruption and intimidation of juries as 'violent, tyrannical and contrary to the liberty and custom of England'.[10] Its significance is evident from the fact that ten editions were published in English before the end of the 17th century. Maitland, the great constitutional lawyer, said that nobody should write about Elizabeth's reign without consulting it. It is a remarkable work since it was written by Smith from memory without a single book or lawyer to consult. The book was not published until 1583, some six years after his death. Later scholars have argued that the book anticipated the Parliamentary revolution in Stuart times. He described England as a 'mixed monarchy' and stated that the 'most high and absolute power of the realm of England consisteth in Parliament'. Although he did not set out to challenge the Crown, the Stuart assertion of the divine right of kings found no support in the book.

The book incorporated whole chapters of William Harrison's *Description of England*. It seems that both Smith and Harrison contemplated the incorporation of both their manuscripts in the unrealised project of Reginald Wolfe, the Queen's Printer and Master of the Stationer's Company for a 'Universal Cosmography of the Whole World'. In fact *Description of England* was published in 1577 as part of Holinshed's *Chronicle*. Harrison (1534-93) who was born in London, became Rector of Radwinter in 1559 and Vicar of Wimbish in 1571. He was buried at St George's Windsor, where he became a canon towards the end of his life.

Despite his literary achievements, Smith was bitter about his diplomatic exile and complained vociferously to Cecil. He then apologised for his 'rough tongue and rude manners'. He knew that his main hope of reinstatement at court depended on Cecil, whom he regarded as his one faithful friend at court. Prominent amongst his political enemies was Throckmorton, who enjoyed a close relationship with Dudley. At last in April 1566 Smith was recalled, to be replaced by Sir Philip Hoby. On leaving the French court he was given plate, 'all gilt and in twelve cases', consisting of 'two flagons, three salts with covers, three standing cups, six bowls with a cover, two basins and ewers and twelve trenchers'.[11] He was not particularly grateful and complained of the workmanship except for one basin and ewer, which 'two be not unpretty'.

He returned to Essex and remained at home, seemingly forgotten. The management of Smith's estates had suffered, although Cecil had kindly advised and assisted Lady Philippa in her 'widowed state'. The Bishop of Carlisle had been troublesome and hardly any of his deanery money had come his way. Despite all that Smith was wealthy enough to plunge into his building plans for Hill Hall. In March 1567 Elizabeth recalled Smith to Court and sent him back to France to make a formal request under the Treaty of Cateau-Cambrésis for the return of Calais. Smith went through the motions. He made a demand for the city outside its gates with trumpets and heralds, but all knew that it was an empty gesture. He also delivered a formal speech at the French Court. Catherine tersely rejected the request and Smith returned empty-handed to England. It did not help Smith's cause that Norris, the new ambassador, wrote to Elizabeth that Smith was but lightly regarded in France, and that the mission had failed because of Smith's incompetence.

6
The Elizabethan Secretary of State
'My fault is plainness and that I cannot dissemble enmity or pleasure'

Retirement in Essex

For the next four years until the spring of 1571, Smith stayed in virtual retirement in Essex although he still sought office. Despite Cecil's efforts on his behalf, Elizabeth remained deaf to his pleas. Smith busied himself with his estate and local affairs. He presented Walden with a large cup of silver in a special ceremony.[1] He also served as a justice of the peace on all Essex commissions from July 1567 to October 1570. He served in the Ongar and Epping divisions. In the summer of 1570 he was involved in the collection of the subsidy in the county.

Amongst the matters brought to Smith as a JP were two cases of witchcraft, which are worth relating as they reveal much of the popular thinking of the day. The wife of one Malter of Theydon Mount was examined in April 1570. She had told her husband that he was bewitched. As a remedy she made a trivet of elder and hazel with a fire below. She got her husband, who was not well in his wits, to kneel down and say certain prayers to be delivered. He had a sheep shearing at this time and two of his sheep and a sow died. Another witness deposed that her mistress, a farmer's wife, declined to bring some sprats from London for the Goodwife Malter. The maid then related how a bird had fluttered amongst her milking pans and would not be driven away. Then it went into the cheese loft whence it emerged as a toad. Then for five weeks they were unable to produce any butter. But when the milk was taken to a neighbour's house it produced butter as before.

In the case of Anne Vicars, Smith took evidence in May. A woman deposed that three years ago she was taken with a strange illness, her body was disfigured, her lips swollen and black, and she almost went out of her wits. The woman went to see one Cobham of Rochford, who told her that she was indeed bewitched by Anne Vicars, and told her of the words used when they fell out. Cobham promised that as long as he lived Anne would have no power over her. But shortly after he died, she fell again into disease. Another woman of Stapleford Abbots said that three years ago, she was coming from Romford Market with Anne Vicars when she had cast up her nose and declared that she smelt a whore or a thief. Then she spied the wife of one Ingersole, whom she caught up with and cast her apron over her and made many crosses and prayers. The deponent protested that Ingersole's wife was an honest woman. But Ingersole's wife fell very sick and lost one of her eyes with a stroke.

Maud Ingersole said that Anne Vicars' daughter did sell wood that was assigned in the common to her. Maud forbade her to do so, whereupon Anne Vicars fell out with her and wished that she might not be delivered of the child with which she was pregnant. This happened on the Monday. On the Thursday she lost her eye. Agnes Combres testified that the supposed witch fell out with her and fell a cursing and banning at her and wished her eyes out. Whereupon within two days she fell down as dead, extremely sick and barely recovered. And since that time she had marvellous pains in her eyes. There were further depositions. It seems that Smith committed these tiresome and deluded women to jail.[2]

Smith was much occupied with his estate. He made an inventory of all his possessions at Ankerwicke in September 1569. A rental survey of the Theydon Mount manor was made.

He substantially rebuilt Hill Hall in 1567 and 1568. His interest in things architectural is evident from the twelve important books on architecture in his library. He had grandiose plans for an even more splendid and imposing mansion round the existing Hill Hall. He wrote to Heneage, 'I am altogether the countryman… All other pleasures be for times and places; that is never out of season, the contemplation of nature and the marvellous works of God'.[3] These building projects all required a constant flow of ready cash. Smith nourished two schemes to make money: The first was for making copper from iron on a large scale; and the second for the conquest and settlement of Ireland under a company owned and directed by himself (see Chapter 7).

Recall to Court

But after an absence of four years, Smith found himself recalled to Court in March 1571 as a member of the Privy Council. Throckmorton had died in February 1571, Walsingham had been sent to France as ambassador, and Cecil, now Lord Burghley, needed assistance in the heavy role of Secretary. Smith was appointed Secretary in July 1572. The Puritans were pressing for a more radical reform of the Church in a Calvinistic direction. Smith was thought to be well suited to act as a moderate intermediary with Parliament. There was much suspicion of internal plots and foreign interference in England's affairs. Elizabeth had been excommunicated by the Pope in 1570 following the northern rebellions in 1569.[4] The House of Commons responded by seeking to extend the list of offences to be regarded as high treason. A bill was introduced for the compulsory attendance at church to include communion. Parliament urged the reform of canon law 'to have all things brought to the purity of the primitive church'. Smith, alarmed at these radical proposals, temporised by suggesting that the bill be considered first by the bishops.

Plots and Treasons

In April 1571 reports reached Burghley of a plot to seize power and proclaim Mary Queen of Scots as monarch. Mary had fled Scotland after the scandal of Darnley's murder.[5] In England she was promptly placed under house arrest. The Spanish Government had crushed the Protestant revolt in the Netherlands, and Philip II turned his attention to England. Ridolfi, an Italian financier, was behind the plot. The aim was to marry Mary to the Duke of Norfolk, Elizabeth's second cousin. Smith found that he was 'the one that was most employed in the searching of the late treasons' and became the principal inquisitor.[6] At the end of May Smith was assisted by Dr Thomas Wilson, another civil lawyer and Master of Requests. They wrote long confidential reports to Burghley on the results of their enquiries.

In August 1571 Smith was present to wait upon the Queen at Audley End in the course of one of her royal progresses around the nation. Strype describes this quaintly:

The Queen was at Audley-End in August this year. Here Sir Thomas Smith now was: perhaps repairing thither to congratulate her Majesty's coming so near Walden his native town, or to wait upon her for some favour for that place, or otherwise.[7]

There were rumours that gold was being sent to Lord Harris in Scotland to assist in the cause of Mary Queen of Scots. At the end of September, to get to the bottom of the conspiracy, Smith interrogated Higford, the Duke of Norfolk's secretary, and his agents, Barker and Bannister. Higford confessed that the Duke had instructed him to send £600 to

Lord Harris. Smith wrote to Burghley to state that he had enough evidence to arrest Norfolk. Burghley ordered one Sadler to ride through the night and arrest Norfolk at Howard Place. At 5 o'clock the following evening Sadler and Smith escorted Norfolk to the Tower. Smith gave Norfolk a full written statement of the charges. Smith and Wilson searched the Duke's rooms at Howard Place, and found the cipher used for messages to Mary hidden under tiles in the roof. For several days they remorselessly questioned Norfolk and his servants, whilst resisting the Queen's demands that torture be used against Duke's servants. The Queen wrote to Smith and Wilson, 'Neither Barker nor Bannister, the Duke of Norfolk's men, have uttered their knowledge, neither will discover without torture … We warrant you to cause them both or either of them to be brought to the rack.'[8] Both men begged 'revocation from this unpleasant and painful toil', but were forced to concede to the royal command.[9] Further information came in, and by the end of September all the details of the plot were in the Queen's hands. So Thomas Howard, 4th Duke of Norfolk, was brought to trial and executed in the Tower, where his father, the 3rd Duke, had been imprisoned throughout the reign of Edward VI.

Return to France

Smith's role in the affair was not finished, since the Queen considered that Smith was the man best qualified to explain to the French Court the reasons for her moving against Mary and Norfolk. He was to reveal Mary's treacherous negotiations with the Papacy and Spain. Mary had shown herself 'our open mortal enemy'. He was to explain that Mary was expecting 6,000 troops from Spain, and that she 'had made full determination in no wise to be directed by the French King although she would pretend otherwise'.[10]

Smith was appointed as joint ambassador with Sir Francis Walsingham, who was later to become Elizabeth's spymaster-in-chief. The increasing influence of Coligny, the Huguenot leader at Court, raised hopes of an Anglo-French alliance against Spain. Elizabeth allowed her envoys to raise expectations of a possible marriage with the Duke of Anjou as a bait in the negotiations. Walsingham fell ill in September, so Smith took over the negotiations. Religion was a big obstacle in the negotiations. Elizabeth would not allow Anjou to remain a Roman Catholic in his public role. However, it was conceded that he might have private exercise of his religion, provided that he used no mass or other rights repugnant to the word of God. If Anjou would not accept these terms, then Smith was instructed to abandon the marriage project.

Smith had a bad crossing of the Channel and suffered nightmares. He wrote to ask Anne Heneage to interpret his dreams, which all reflected a high state of anxiety. Anne was the wife of Smith's neighbour, Thomas Heneage (1532-1595) of Copt Hall, Epping, who rose to be Treasurer in the court of Queen Elizabeth. On 4 January Smith reported the Norfolk plot to the French King, the Queen Mother and the King's younger brothers, the Dukes of Anjou and Alençon. He stated that all the confessions in their written statements had been made without torture or torment applied, which he assured the French was contrary to both the laws and custom of England.[11] Smith was being dishonest since he knew perfectly well that he had resorted to torture at the insistence of the Queen. Catherine and Anjou responded by insisting that Anjou must enjoy full freedom in the practice of his faith.

On a happier note, Smith wrote home to his wife with detailed instructions for the new garden at Theydon Mount. 'If you have had such weather you will have had good time to carry much dung into the garden …' He then mentions red roses, pear and apple trees, gooseberries, mustard seed, hops, white damasines, and damask roses. He also boasted of the hospitality that he had received in France:

Nine or ten cooks in my kitchen, butlers, victualers, and officers of the King's house appointed to serve me. Of meat, wine, bread, candles, plate and all such things as if I were a young prince, and all of the King's charges. Minstrels and music more than I would have …[12]

He was allowed 'two messes of meat so well furnished that it passeth reason and all exquisite dishes that can be got'. But he went on to say that he abhorred too much meat and longed for 'a good piece of court beef and mustard, a cowsheel and a piece of ling and sodden oysters, instead of all these pheasants and partridges … and young peacocks and all other such fine meats, covered and seethened with lard'.[13]

After the rejection of Elizabeth's conditions by Anjou, Smith sought to persuade the Queen of the claims of Alençon, whom he described in extravagant terms without much regard for Elizabeth's feelings. This did not endear him to the Queen. But Smith was far less isolated than in his previous embassy. He used his relations as messengers. Nephew John Wood acted as secretary for part of the time. Gabriel Cawode, son of the Queen's printer, who married Smith's niece carried many dispatches. He also used Robert Beale, a young man with 'excellent gifts', and Thomas Cheveley, 'as a child brought up with me'. Smith's son was also employed although mainly occupied in preparations for Smith's Irish venture.

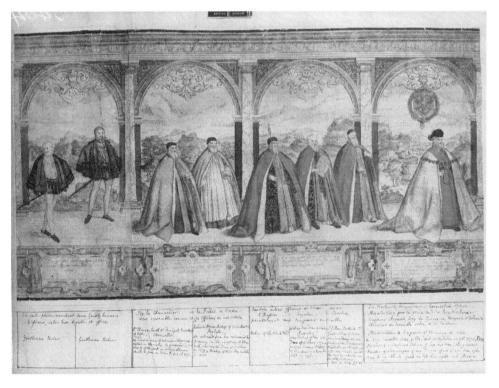

Figure 31: The Procession of the Knights of the Garter, 1576 by M. Gheeraerts – Sir Thomas Smith as Chancellor is depicted third from left in this picture from the National Portrait Gallery.

Smith turned his attention to negotiations on a French alliance. The three main issues were: mutual aid if attacked; the settlement of Scotland; and the establishment in France of a staple for the English cloth trade. Smith reported that he was handicapped in his mission because the French set much store by titles. This far from subtle hint was rewarded when he was informed that he was to be made Chancellor of the Order of the Garter (Fig. 31). This brought high honour but little profit. The negotiations began to come apart when the French revived their concern for Mary. Smith responded by insisting on mutual aid being included openly in the treaty, although Elizabeth had offered a secret commitment. During a lull in the proceedings, Smith took the opportunity to visit the Huguenot, Vidame de Chartres, who was engaged in experiments in the distilling of 'waters'. He also read one of the books of Raymond Lully, the Majorcan writer and philosopher, with great interest.

But Elizabeth's further instructions were delayed. Smith fell ill with vomiting and complaining of the bitter cold. He complained that in his bedchamber he could make no fire. He underwent bloodletting. In an angry critical mood he wrote to Burghley that Elizabeth would 'with irresolution make all princes to understand that there is no certainty in Her Majesty nor Her Council but dalliance and fooling of time'.[14] Elizabeth was a great temporiser, who lived by the maxim, 'video et taceo' ('I see and say nothing'). Everything was going wrong. The Council complained of his long letters and irrelevancies. He was anxious about his Irish venture; the copper works in Poole were losing money; he was worried about his estates; and over his stills and experiments, which he had left in the care of Mr Parsons. He wrote to his wife: 'I pray you give Mr Parsons the £5 and let them lack no coals or other things necessary. I must needs make much of that to the which, next God, I perceive I owe my life and my health as this last winter I have had good experience …'[15]

Smith rebuked Parsons for not answering his letters; even the King and Queen of France did that. He complained to Burghley that he was old and wished to come home. But he and Walsingham were stuck with negotiations. Eventually, agreement was reached and a defensive league against Spain was sealed in the Treaty of Blois, on 19 April 1572. Nothing came of a staple port in France for the English cloth trade. England and France did agree to try to pacify the warring parties in Scotland. This was the peak of Smith's power and influence. He was invited to dine with the French King accompanied only by the Dukes of Anjou and Alençon, and by Walsingham and the Lord Admiral Clinton. They were entertained with music, Italian comedy and acrobatics. A religious ceremony was held at St Germain's Church near the Louvre. Smith was presented with 472 ounces of silver valued at ten shillings an ounce, mainly vases and collars. He told his wife that he would be home with her 'before all your roses be done'; he told Parsons that he would soon be home to 'set all my stills in order'.[16] He was home by the first week in July and Elizabeth made him sole Secretary in succession to Burghley, who became Lord High Treasurer.

First Secretary

From 1572 Smith handled the tasks of First Secretary with a caution and lack of initiative 'which tells its own story of an increasing awareness of age and the abandonment of real political ambition'.[17] He seemed content to become Burghley's confidential clerk. Burghley accepted Smith's precious 'bottles of water' for his ailments. Raw alcohol appears to be the main ingredient. He was happy to have Burghley between him and the Queen. 'My fault is plainness and that I cannot dissemble enmity or pleasure.' He believed in straight dealing: 'For that though playing under the Board served sometimes the jugglers, yet we saw by proof in friendship it lasted not but brought inconvenience'.[18] He did not like women very much and thought them 'wayward' and frivolous'. His letters to his wife contain something of a hectoring tone. He seemed to take no interest in what women wore or what music they played.

He found the Queen exasperating for her lack of decision-making and her endless delays. Elizabeth was unwilling to sign anything until she had discussed matters with Burghley. In March 1574 he found Elizabeth in the morning 'fully resolved to go forward with my Lord of Essex's plan without any going back'. By evening she had decided not to proceed until she had discussed things with Burghley. He complained that all he wanted was 'a little rest. I am thoroughly weary, both in mind and body and can scarcely endure any longer.'[19] He regretted the time spent with the Queen on progress:

Lay at Theobolds, my Lord Treasurer's house three days. Now is merry at my Lord Keeper's house called Gorhambury besides St Albans and tomorrow goeth to Dunstable and the next day to Woodstock and endeth Her progress at Windsor the 23rd of September.[20]

It was all a waste of time. Work was piling up but 'we play at tables and dance and keep Christmas'.[21] Highway robbery was proving a problem, and Smith drew up a proclamation which made it illegal to carry about any weapon on pain of imprisonment. Noblemen and 'upright gentlemen' were exempted from this provision. Smith did exert himself on Ireland, and encouraged the Queen to back the Irish expeditions. In 1573 Elizabeth was prevailed to send the Earl of Essex to conquer Antrim, but she drew back after her first decision. She refused to sign the letters for the Earl's departure and the Privy Council was unenthusiastic. After an exhausting conference with the Queen, he reported to Burghley that the Queen 'still harped' on about the risks and the costs.

The move for a more radical reform of the Church aroused no enthusiasm in Smith. But he had no love for Catholics, whom he suspected of disloyalty. In 1573 he reported that 'the commission to seek out conjurors and mass-mongers' had done very well and uncovered 'a foul knot of papistical justices of the peace and of massing priests'.[22] But he did not favour more penal laws against Catholics. Instead, they should be sent to Italy and 'let them live by sucking the Pope's teats', as he crudely put it.[23] He disliked Puritan fanatics, and their 'prophesyings' seemed ignorant and seditious. When Parliament was prorogued from 30 June 1572 to February 1576, Smith was relieved and felt that he could get on with the business of government without parliamentary interference.

Massacre of St Bartholomew's Day

The whole country was shocked by the news of the massacre of St Bartholomew's Day on 24 August 1572. Many French Huguenots had gathered in Paris for the marriage of the Catholic Princess Margaret to the Protestant Henry of Navarre. Catherine of Medici, for 30 years the effective ruler of France, ordered the assassination of Admiral Coligny and the killing of his Huguenot supporters. The massacre in Paris was followed by massacres in other French towns. As the Guises swept back into power in France with their pro-Spanish policies, Smith saw the wreck of all that he had sought to achieve as Ambassador. He wrote apocalyptically to Walsingham:

'I would that you were at home out of that country so contaminated with innocent blood that the sea cannot look upon but to prognosticate the wrath and vengeance of God.'[24]

Slowly the diplomatic breach was healed and Smith was involved with sending the Earl of Worcester to France for the baptism of Charles IX's infant daughter. Walsingham even raised again the question of a possible marriage of Elizabeth to the Duke of Alençon.

Fig. 32. Sir Francis Walsingham.

Smith feared domestic consequences from the French contagion. He thought that Elizabeth's reluctance to move against Mary Queen of Scots was weak. He considered that she should be executed. Furthermore, if the Queen married, 'traitorous hearts' would be discouraged, and doubts and fears about the succession would cease. His new-found friendship with Walsingham was a great source of pleasure (Fig. 32). They had interests in common. In December 1572 both interrupted their talk of state affairs to talk about a new star, which had appeared in the heavens. Smith had a passion for astrology, which he could not throw off, and regarded himself as a passionate Sagittarian. He kept Walsingham very well briefed in France, and agitated Elizabeth for Walsingham's return when he had had enough of the ambassadorship. Walsingham returned home in April 1573. At that time, Smith was made Keeper of the Privy Seal. When Smith fell ill in December, Elizabeth appointed Walsingham Second Secretary and he and Smith worked closely together for two years.

A letter to Burghley on 17 July 1574 illustrates Smith's busy schedule. He had received letters from Burghley, 'being at my Lord Chamberlain's office at 7 o'clock at night'. Immediately he had sought an audience with the Queen to discuss them, settled Burghley's requests, drafted the bill for which Burghley had asked, and settled down to reply to him at 10 o'clock at night. Before 8 o'clock the next morning the letters to Burghley had gone and a long despatch to Wilson on the same matter had been written and sent.[25] No wonder that Smith complained 'I have neither eyes to see nor legs to stand upon'.[26]

Parliament sat again in the spring of 1576. This meant more work for ministers. Smith was responsible for steering through the House an 'Act for the Maintenance of the Universities'. Its provisions show every sign of being drafted by Smith himself. The main clause stated that one third of the rents due to the colleges was to be paid in corn or malt at a fixed price or under if the market rate was low. The Act protected the colleges from the worst effects of the steady rise in commodity prices. The price of corn was fixed at 6s 8d per quarter or under and malt at 5s a quarter or under. It was the same device that Smith had introduced into leases as Provost of Eton, whereby the college gained and saved above £200 per year. The Bill was linked with another in which it was sought to stop the sale of fellowships in the university. This Bill went through the Commons and Lords but was vetoed by the Queen.

Smith was also involved with committees looking at the debasement of the coinage, the trade in cloth and wine and other matters but to no great purpose. He became desperately ill. Dewar suggests that he had cancer of the throat. In March he left the Court and went to his brother's house. He consulted physicians who gave him little hope. He drew up his will. 'For what pleasure can a man have of my years when he cannot speak as he would.'[27] Various remedies were tried to no avail. He left London and went home to Hill Hall 'where I trust to leave my sickness or my life... It is a matter to be done with the cure of hand of a surgeon and to be cut away that doth let [i.e. prevent] my speech.'[28] But no such surgeon with the necessary skill was to be found.

As summer came Smith found the energy to look over his earlier writings and he searched out his work on Roman coins and the pay of Roman soldiers. He revived his interest in Cambridge University. He looked into the teaching of civil law and complained that young scholars had little of the exact learning of earlier days. He encouraged his cousin, Gabriel Harvey, the Saffron Walden-born writer and scholar, and sought to further his career.[29] Harvey (1545-1630) was the eldest son of a ropemaker from Saffron Walden (Fig. 33). He matriculated at Christ's Cambridge in 1566 and was elected a fellow of Pembroke College Cambridge in 1570. Here he formed a lasting friendship with Edmund Spenser. He wanted to be known as the inventor of the English hexameter and he wished to impose Latin rules upon English verse. Harvey was also a proficient wordsmith, who is credited with the

invention of words such as 'jovial', 'conscious', 'idiom', 'notoriety' and 'rascality', Later he entered into a furious argument with Thomas Nashe, the pamphleteer and poet. Nashe mocked Harvey, 'who goes twitching and hopping in our language like a man running upon quagmires, up the hill in one syllable and down the dale in the other'.[30] Much later Nashe produced a satirical tract entitled 'Have with you to Saffron Walden' (1596), which depicted Harvey rushing to the toilet at the thought of Nashe producing yet another pamphlet.

Fig. 33. Gabriel Harvey.

The quarrel between Harvey and Nashe was to lie in the future after Smith's death. For the present Smith sent Harvey money, recommended him for his fellowship and took Harvey's sister into his wife's household. Harvey was grateful and on Smith's death wrote a long Latin eulogy: *Gabriel Harveii Valdinatis Smithus vel Musarum Lachrymae pro Obitu Clarissimi Thomas Smyth.* On Smith's death, Harvey, who seems to have been constitutionally quarrelsome, became involved in an acrimonious dispute with Andrew Perne, Master of Peterhouse and preacher at Smith's funeral, over the bequest of some of Smith's books.

Smith had earlier founded two fellowships and two scholarships at Queens' and urged the College to appoint his nephew Clement, George's third son, to a vacant fellowship. But the Queen had her own candidate and angrily told the College to proceed according to her wishes. Later Clement was appointed to another vacancy. Smith proceeded to wind up his affairs. He made an inventory of all his books. All his belongings were brought from the Court at Greenwich to his London house and then carried to Hill Hall, where they were duly added to the inventory. All his apparel was listed, as was his plate and even the fish in the fishponds. In February he had drawn up an indenture disposing of all his lands during and after Philippa's lifetime. In April he made his will. In September Smith travelled to Bath to take the waters. But he got no relief and wanted to go home and finish his mansion house at Theydon Mount.

7
The Merchant Venturer

'Great Crakes and Promises'

The Copper Venture

In between his public duties as a Secretary of State, Smith involved himself in the 1570s with his own speculative ventures in Ireland and in copper. The motivation for both schemes was financial but they were to bring nothing but worry, failure and financial disaster. It began with William Medley, a persuasive young man, who convinced Smith that he could make copper by boiling iron in vitriol (sulphuric acid). He conducted experiments at Canon Row. Because vitriol was expensive and imported into England, Medley said that he had found a way of manufacturing vitriol. Copper was in great demand for the ordnance. Smith got Sir Humphrey Gilbert, the navigator and future founder of Newfoundland, to join him in the copper venture. They each put up £100 for Medley in Winchelsea. Then Medley moved to Poole where he received another advance of £200 from Smith and Gilbert. When Smith moved to France he expected Gilbert to supervise Medley, but Gilbert remained in London trusting Medley's 'great crakes and promises'. Smith raged that Medley was leading Gilbert by the nose, and that he was 'too much assoted upon Mr Medley'.[1]

Medley told Smith that he had found the right earths but that permission must be obtained from Lord Mountjoy, who had a monopoly on the working of earths for the production of alum or copper. Lady Mountjoy agreed to let her Poole house to Smith, Gilbert and Medley for £400 so that they could share in the working of the earths. Medley delayed progress because his name was not on the lease, and then because it was missing from the patent. On return from France, Smith hurried down to Poole to inspect progress. He found no copper, the works abandoned, and £62 owing to workmen. Gilbert had gone off on an expedition to Flushing; Medley was nowhere to be found.

Two years later Medley again approached Smith claiming that he had found the perfect ingredients in Anglesey, and that Smith should enlist the financial support of Lord Burghley and the Earl of Leicester, as well as Gilbert. Smith was naïve enough to be convinced of the money-making opportunities. On 28 January 1575 Smith got the patent of the Society approved. It was called the Society of the New Art. The Queen was to be given a share of the profits and the Society could dig, open and work any mines anywhere in the country. Medley, the perfect conman, was advanced large sums. He then stalled and delayed and asked for more money to settle old debts. He put all the blame on Gilbert. Smith and Gilbert each lost over a thousand pounds. No more was heard of the scheme and a few years later Medley appeared in court as a bankrupt.

The Irish Colony

Ireland was a bigger venture and a greater failure. The Lord Deputy, the Queen's representative in Ireland, exercised only nominal control over the 'pure Irish', who lived under the fitful leadership of the various clan chieftains. Revenue gathered from the land barely paid for the small garrison of soldiers maintained in Dublin. Ireland's attachment to

Rome meant that Ireland remained a constant backdoor threat to England. In June 1565 Smith wrote of Ireland to Cecil; 'For this two hundred years not one hath taken the right way to make that country either subject or profitable'.[2] Its conquest was 'the most honourable and princely enterprise that Her Majesty might take in hand'. He later wrote:

To my mind it needeth nothing more than to make colonies. To augment our tongue, our laws and our religion in that Isle, which three be the true bands of the commonwealth whereby the Romans conquered and kept long time a great part of the world.[3]

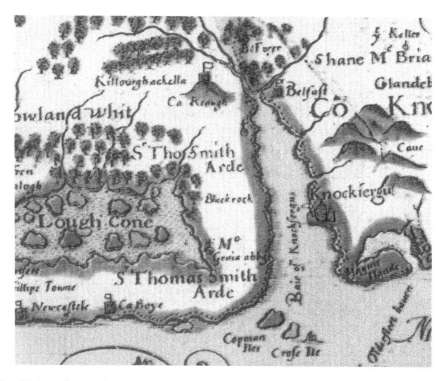

Fig. 34. Map showing the Irish colony proposed by Smith with his claim for the Arde near Belfast.

Various attempts had earlier been made to colonise Ireland; Sir Thomas Croft had tried in the 1550s and Sir Henry Sydney in the 1560s. In 1571 Smith petitioned the Queen for a grant of lands in Ireland, which he and a company formed by him would conquer 'at their own charges and perils' in order to 'make the same civil and peopled with natural Englishmen born'. He produced a broadsheet appealing for subscriptions. This has been described as the first piece of sustained argument for overseas colonisation to be published in England, and the first direct printed publicity in England for any business venture.[4] It took the form of an imaginary dialogue between individuals. It was a plan for an Irish colony in the Ards Peninsula lying to the south of Belfast between the Irish Sea and Strangford Lough (Fig. 34). England was over-populated 'with few dwellings empty'. So English footmen who joined the expedition would receive 300 acres of land paying only one penny an acre rent. Horsemen would get double that amount. Loyal Irishmen would serve as labourers. A port would be built and the Queen's permission sought to export corn to England, France and Spain.

It was sent out nominally under the hand of Thomas Smith junior, Sir Thomas Smith's illegitimate son, whose leadership qualities were extolled. The Queen was furious that this broadsheet was published without her prior consent. Smith was also rebuked by the Privy Council. Elizabeth did eventually approve the venture; letters patent granted 360,000 acres in the Great and Little Ards region to Smith and his son. But the whole venture was put at risk when Smith was sent off to France. His son began to collect volunteers for the expedition. He wrote to Leicester and Burghley and others soliciting their help. Burghley paid nearly £340 for the promise of 'twenty ploughlands' to be allotted in the Ards. But opposition came from Ireland. The Lord Deputy, Fitzwilliam, an Essex neighbour of Smith, was against the project as he rightly suspected that it would stir the Irish into rebellion. Sir Brian O'Neill complained that the Queen had given away his lands in the grant. Sir Brian McFelim complained that lands held by his family for fourteen generations had been given to the Smiths.

The expedition was going nowhere. From March to August the volunteers hung around in Liverpool causing trouble. The son Thomas was incapable of organising and controlling the venture. He was reprimanded by his father: 'A wavering reed and irresolute mind bringeth no stable thing to pass.'[5] He told him that, unless he got things properly managed, 'I will hereafter take you for a fantastical fool and give you a long Adieu'.[6] John Wood, his sister's son, who was acting as secretary to Smith tried to intercede but Smith told him that his son acted as if 'I had a bottomless purse or mine for him to spend at his pleasure'.[7] Thomas annoyed the Lord Deputy Fitzwilliam, and made matters worse by borrowing wheat from Fitzwilliam and £100 from Fitzwilliam's wife to pay for his expenses when he arrived in Dublin.

When Smith returned from France as Secretary in July 1572, permission was given for the expedition to sail. When Fitzwilliam asked for 800 more soldiers for the garrison, he was blandly informed by Elizabeth that Smith's expedition would deal with any trouble. By August many of the 700 to 800 men recruited by Thomas had drifted away, and he landed in Dublin with only 100 men. They soon ran into trouble with the local Irish headed by O'Neill. There was no discipline. Reinforcements slipped away for the more profitable occupation of piracy in the Channel. Then on 20 October 1573 Thomas Smith junior himself was murdered by some Irish servants in his household. The Earl of Essex, leading his own expedition into Ireland, reported the news to the Privy Council. He said that George, Smith's brother, had witnessed the murder and was on his way home to report. There was horror at home. Smith was thoroughly shaken. He had invested his hopes in this illegitimate son of his youth, especially as his second marriage had proved childless. 'The hapless Thomas Smith was at once the victim of his father's innovative but untested colonial ideas and his own ignorance of Irish affairs.'[8]Smith collapsed and was brought home to Essex where he lay distraught for several weeks. But he rallied and threw his efforts into a second attempt at colonisation.

A Colonial Constitution

In December 1574 Smith drew up detailed plans, which were nothing less than a complete blueprint for the government of a colony. It included plans for courts leet and courts baron. He proposed a principal city to be called 'Elizabetha'. All settlers were to live in settled towns, not isolated homesteads. The town plan included a market place set up in the middle of blocks of rectangular streets and a large space left around them for a good wide highway running around the town's defences. He drew up detailed regulations for farming. None were to be excused for not having cultivated their land; there would be fines for untilled land. All goods were to be exported and imported through the one port. He drew up a quasi-military form of government under a Deputy-Colonel, supposing that until the colony could establish peace and order there would be a state of half war and half peace.

One-tenth of the adventurers were to form an Advisory Common Council, which was in turn to choose a Privy Council empowered to administer all military matters under the Deputy-Colonel. At a time of crisis the Colonel or his deputy could call out half the soldiers of the colony. The soldiers were expected to support themselves in the field for 40 days. After 40 days these soldiers would be sent home and replaced by the other half. Those at home could escape service if they would pay to support those already in the field for a further 40 days. Failure to report for duty would be punished. Spoils taken in battle were to be divided equally among the soldiers with the officers having a larger share. For the first two years the colonists were not to hold banquets, give feasts or entertain one another. 'Two things do I wish most especially avoided now at the beginning of this colony, superfluity of fare or delicacies and excess of apparel.'[9]

Armed with this blueprint Smith again appealed for support. The ever obliging Burghley put money into the venture as did John Thynne of Longleat. Sir John Berkeley of Gloucestershire invested over £1,000, and there were 20 indentures of supporters who each promised over £400. Edmund Verney was pledged for 20 horse and 40 footmen. Brother George and his three sons were put in charge of the campaign.

The Earl of Essex at Claneboy in Ulster was struggling with Irish uprisings. In March 1574 Elizabeth demanded that Smith send more forces to Ards or be prepared to sell out his interests to the Earl of Essex. In August nearly 200 men sailed under Smith's brother, George, and Jerome Brett. They achieved some success at first. But in November an Irish rebellion drove the settlers right out of Ards. Brett disobeyed Smith and quarrelled with George. Smith begged Fitzwilliam to dismiss Brett. By the late spring of 1575 it was clear that the latest expedition was a complete failure. Smith formally requested Essex to take over all his lands in Ireland. In 1579 Smith's heir and nephew, Sir William Smith, tried to revive the Smith claims in Ards, but he met with hostility and was recalled to Dublin in disgrace.

In Walden the Strachey family, who lived in The Close, on the corner of the High Street and Castle Street, remained close friends of the Smiths for generations (Fig. 35). Thirty years after Smith's death, the grandson of his oldest friend, William Strachey, the first secretary of the new American colony of Virginia returned to publish his account of the new colony and to write his *Laws, Divine, Moral and Martial* for Virginia. It is a tantalising question as to whether young Strachey gained his enthusiasm for colonial enterprises and understanding of constitutional law from the Irish dreams of Smith at Theydon Mount.

Fig. 35. The Close, Saffron Walden, home of the Stracheys, close friends of the Smiths.

8
The Lasting Legacy

'Piously and sweetly slept in the Lord'

Fig. 36. Rear view of Hill Hall south range which now faces the M25. Pevsner says the external large Tuscan columns are a unique occurrence in Europe.

Hill Hall

The present mansion house of Hill Hall at Theydon Mount, though added to in the 18th century, is Smith's architectural legacy (Fig. 36). For a long time it was neglected in the history of Tudor architecture. Professor Pevsner wrote: 'Hill Hall is, in spite of its moderate size, one of the most important earlier Elizabethan houses in the country. This fact is on the whole too little appreciated .One or two of its features are quite exceptional and of high architectural significance.'[1] It seems that Smith was solely responsible for the design since he had a passion for building and architecture. He possessed Latin and French books on the subject, as well as six editions of *De Architectura*, the famous work of Marcus Vitruvius Pollio, the Roman architect and engineer, active in the first century BC. These were bought in France, not being well known in England. Pevsner points out that the classical motif used in the courtyard at Hill Hall can be found in Vitruvius.[2] There are striking resemblances to Hill Hall in the Château of Bournazel, 75 metres north-east of Toulouse, and in the Hôtel d'Assézat at Toulouse, both built in the 1550s. Smith spent time recuperating at Toulouse and seems to have been much influenced by these two buildings.

Hill Hall had its origins before the Norman Conquest, when it was owned by a Saxon called Godric. The first house was built on the same site in the early 13th century. The house was essentially a timber-framed manor, which grew haphazardly. It included a stone solar raised on an undercroft. After Smith acquired the property he began extending it to the east on the site of a forecourt and gardens. His house was partly of brick and partly timber-framed. The bricks were set in loam and not mortar, and they soon began to fail. Smith decided on a total reconstruction. In 1567-68 he rebuilt the north and west ranges 'more strongly and splendidly'. Four years later in 1572-73 the remaining sides of the courtyard were rebuilt. At the time of Smith's death in 1577 further building work was under way, presumably on the north-west range which contained some of the domestic quarters.

Fig. 37. Hill Hall inner courtyard showing Doric and Ionic columns.

The main feature of the house is the inner courtyard, which has three orders of columns on three floors (Fig. 37). The columns are Doric on the ground floor, Ionic on the second floor and Corinthian on the attic dormers. The external front of the house has two big projecting blocks at each corner, against which stand two gigantic Tuscan columns. The handling of this 'giant order' in the front of the house is, according to Professor Pevsner, 'a unique occurrence in England and indeed in Europe'. The internal decoration of the buildings was very ambitious. The north and west ranges were decorated about 1570 with mural paintings, including scenes from the life of Kings Ahaz and Hezekiah, and from the story of Cupid and Psyche (see Frontispiece).[3]

The artist is unknown, but a painter, called Lucas d'Heere, from the Low Countries, was working in England at the time and would have been capable of doing them – Smith would have suggested the subject matter. These paintings survived a disastrous fire in 1969, which destroyed much of the remaining decoration. It is thought that the rapid rebuilding and elaborate decoration of the north and west wings was triggered by the proposed visit of Queen Elizabeth in 1570. However, because of a local outbreak of plague, the royal tour of Essex was cancelled.[4] Smith also planted an orchard specially for apples and pears, and created many fish ponds stocked with carp and tench.

Fig. 38. The Tudor fireplace at Hill Hall, with a bust of Sir Thomas Smith placed over the fireplace probably during the 18th century. Fig. 39. The plaster bust was originally painted in realistic colour and believed to be contemporary with Smith.

Later alterations included the remodelling of the Great Hall at the end of the 17th century, and the rebuilding of the east front around 1714 in the English Baroque style. In the Great Hall over the mantelpiece there is a plaster bust of Sir Thomas Smith, originally painted, which may well be contemporary but has been moved at some time from its original position (Figs. 37, 38).[5] At the end of the 18th century, a north porch was constructed and Humphrey Repton recommended improvements to both the house and the grounds. In 1814 the west front was rebuilt and the wing behind was remodelled.

Hill Hall remained in the hands of the Smith family, later generally known as Smyths, until early in the 20th century. It was purchased in 1923 by Mrs Charles Hunter, a society hostess, who entertained lavishly. After passing through several owners, and being a maternity home and then a billet for RAF officers during World War II, the house was purchased from Lady Hay and converted to a woman's prison, which opened in 1952.[6] In 1969 a major fire gutted the main building. When it came into the possession of English Heritage in 1984 the house was largely a ruin. A programme of restoration costing £2 millions was undertaken to protect and conserve the building. English Heritage has let off apartments in the house whilst retaining the Great Hall and some other rooms.

In 1575 John Cousin, Smith's bailiff, and his wife's servant, Julia Eltropp, testified that they first lived with Sir Thomas and Lady Philippa after their marriage in 1554 at 'Hill Hall'. They lived there with a large household of over 20 servants. The smaller farmhouse, 'Mounthall', was let to Thomas Luther, one of Smith's tenant farmers.[7] After Luther's departure this farmhouse was used from time to time for accommodation and storage by the Smith family. In the last two years of his life Smith did all he could to hurry on the rest of the building. In his will dated 2 April 1576, he stated that after his funeral expenses and main legacies had been met he left the following:

All my chains of gold and one thousand ounces of my gilt plate, and more if need be… to be bestowed upon the finishing of my house at 'Hill Hall' and of a tomb to be made for my wife and me according to the plan and design which I have made by Richard Kirby's advice … and all the brick, timber, chalk, sand and other stuff that I have prepared I would have employed to that use and none other.[8]

It seems that Richard Kirby was an Essex carpenter who may have married one of George's sisters. He was appointed by Smith as 'the Chief Architect and Overseer and Master of my works for the perfecting of my house according to the plan I gave unto him'. He was given by Smith a silver salt, twelve silver spoons and one silver wine cup as a marriage present.

Litigation

Smith had to defend in the courts a claim to the manor, which lasted some 18 months. He only obtained final judgement in November 1576 when it was declared that he had good and lawful title. The case was complicated. In brief it arose from a claim made by Edward Ferrer's widow, Bridget, on behalf of her son Henry. It was claimed that Sir John Hampden (Philippa's first husband) had only conveyed the manor to Philippa for her lifetime and thereafter to his grandson, Edward Ferrers, his wife Bridget and their children. Smith responded that he had made two agreements with Edward Ferrers to secure the property for himself and his heirs.

First in 1555 after Hampden's death, Ferrers had got into financial difficulties and had approached Smith for help. Smith had discharged all Ferrers' debts on consideration of Edward and Bridget assigning the manor to him and his heirs. During Philippa's lifetime Smith agreed to pay them £3 6s 8d a year in 'rent', and after Philippa's death, he and his heirs would pay £30 per annum. This agreement was enrolled in Chancery. However Ferrers did not give up his claim.

On the second occasion in 1559 Ferrers was once more in debt. Again Smith discharged all his debts; Ferrers in return granted to Smith all the yearly rents of the manor and agreed to hand over 'all such deeds … charges … and indentures touching the said manor' which touched on Ferrers' claim. This was meant to extinguish all rights by Ferrers to the manor. Ferrers never delivered these papers. He died in 1564. But Bridget and her son Henry revived the claim. Henry now alleged that there was a Marian deed of enfeoffment, which granted the Hampden lands to the Windsors and the Ferrers. But Henry was unable to produce this deed and judgement was given against him.

Smith's relationship with his wife deteriorated. She seems to have been in league with Ferrers to deny the inheritance to George and his sons. Ferrers did not accept the Chancery judgement and continued to plot even after Smith's death. There is an entry in the Quarter Sessions in Essex for 4 December 1576:

Indictment of Richard Ferrers of the Middle Temple of London, gentleman, and Thomas Mason, servant to Henry Ferrers of Baddesley, Co. Warwick, yeoman, for breaking into the close of Sir Thomas Smyth, Knight, one of the chief Secretaries of the Queen, at Theydon Mount and destroying grass growing there to the value of 10 shillings.[9]

The Death of Sir Thomas Smith

On 12 August 1577, at the age of 62 or 63 years, Sir Thomas Smith died at Hill Hall with his brother George present. Philippa challenged George the very next day over the will. After twelve days a compromise was reached. She abandoned her claim to half the property. In return she received all the stock, stores and crops at Theydon Mount, half of the horses, household stuff and linen in both houses, and a generous settlement of money, jewels and tithes. She also promised to give up to George 'all deeds, evidences, writings, whatsoever ... touching the jointure made to her by John Hampden'. She agreed to furnish three teams of horses and two servants to finish Hill Hall, and to allow the builders to dig earth to make 50,000 bricks, etc. But she did not keep her promise and died the following year, so the house was not speedily finished.

Philippa drew up a will in which she made elaborate bequests to no less than 93 relations, friends and servants. George was not the man to put Theydon Mount in order. The new building was left roofless and neglected. But when his eldest son, William, came back from Ireland, he took over Theydon Mount, paid off his father's debts and put his parents rent free into Ankerwicke. But William quarrelled with his cousin, John Wood. William claimed that the building was still unfinished in 1601 and that Wood had evaded his trust. Sir William Smith married Bridget Fleetwood who bore him three sons and four daughters. He died on 12 December 1626, aged 76.

Fig. 40. Smith's coat of arms with the salamander crest.

William finished the house in accordance with Smith's wishes. He erected a tomb for Smith on the north side of the chancel of St Michael's, Theydon Mount (Figs. 41, 42). It appears to be the one designed by Smith himself. On the altar tomb underneath a semi-circular arch is a full-length effigy of Sir Thomas in full armour, reclining on his right elbow with a loose robe about him. The arms of a Knight of the Garter are on the left sleeve of his robe. His coat of arms has three altars flaming supported by three lions (Fig. 40). Smith changed his crest from an eagle holding in its right claw a pen to that of a salamander. A salamander is a mythical creature supposed to be impervious to fire. This was said to be Smith's thanksgiving for escaping the burnings under Queen Mary. The transcription (translated) reads:

Sir Thomas Smith, Knight, Lord of the Manor, Privy Councillor and Principal Secretary both to King Edward VI and to Queen Elizabeth and their Ambassador to the Greatest Kings, Chancellor of the Noble Order of the Garter, Colonel of Arda and Southern Claneboy in Ireland, honoured even when a youth with the highest title of the Civil Law, a most excellent Orator, Mathematician and Philosopher, very skilful in the Latin, Greek, Hebrew, French, and Italian languages, a friend of the honest and ingenious man, singularly good, serviceable to many, hurtful to none, averse to revenge. In short, remarkable for his wisdom, piety, and integrity and in every part of life whether sick or well prepared for death. When he had completed the sixty-fifth year of his age, he piously and sweetly slept in the Lord at his seat of Mounthalle on the twelfth day of August in the year of his salvation 1577.

Fig. 41. St Michael's Church, Theydon Mount, burial place of Sir Thomas Smith.
Fig. 42. Tomb of Sir Thomas Smith at St Michael's Church, Theydon Mount.

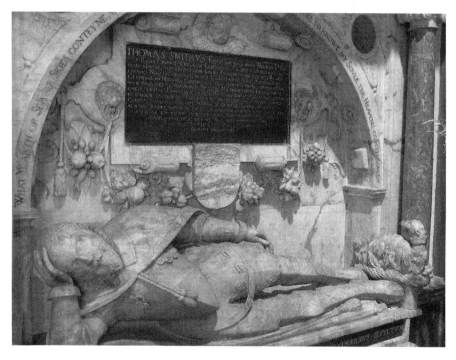

Sir Thomas Smith left behind his second wife Philippa, who died the year after him on 20 June 1578, and was buried beside him. Strype has given us a picture of Smith:

Sir Thomas Smith was of a fair sanguine complexion. His beard which was large and somewhat forked, at the age of thirty-three years, was toward a yellow colour. He had a calm, ingenious countenance, as appears by the picture of him hanging up in the parlour of Hillhall, done, as they say, by Hans Holbein, where he is represented with a round cap on his head, and in a gown, as a civilian: a great ruby ring upon his fore finger, with a curious seal ... laying one of his hands upon a globe, that of his own making, as you may suppose. Underneath the picture is written *Love and Fear*, the two great principles of actions, wherewith God and princes are to be served.[10]

Fig. 43. Portrait of Sir Thomas Smith in Saffron Walden Town Hall based on a picture which used to hang at Hill Hall; right, Smith's original signature on a painting at Hill Hall.

This portrait of Smith allegedly by Holbein used to hang in the hall of Smith's house until Hill Hall was sold in 1932. There are copies in the possession of the Smith-Bowyer family. It is said on the frame to show Smith at the age of 33, but if this is so Holbein would have been dead for three years. It was from this portrait that the 18th century copy of Sir Thomas Smith in the Saffron Town Hall was made (Fig. 43).[11] (See also p.57.)

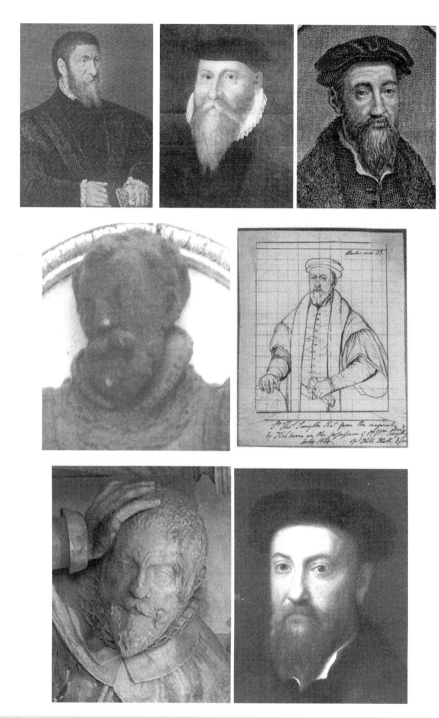

Fig. 44. The many faces of Sir Thomas Smith. Clockwise from top left: painting in Havering Library;   portrait at Queens' College, Cambridge (now known to be 'Customer' Smyth); engraving from Granger Portraits, Vol 3; drawing by Henry Bone; portrait in Saffron Walden Town Hall; recumbent figure on funeral monument at St Michael's Church, Theydon Mount; bust over fireplace at Hill Hall. See also pages 14, 21 and 40.

Appendix

Sir Thomas Smith's Will

Smith returned from Bath in September 1576 and died at Hill Hall in August the following year. In his will he directed that any ambiguity or doubt should be resolved by his cousin Nicholls, Mr Archer and Parson Shaw. George Nicholls, a first cousin of Thomas, lived in Walden. He was a justice of the peace, a reader at the Middle Temple and accounted both 'learned and rich'. Thurston Shaw was Rector of Theydon Mount. Henry Archer was a lawyer from Theydon Garner. A month before his death Smith had drawn up an indenture disposing of all his lands:

> (a) Northamptonshire manors of Oveston and Overton, and Essex properties called Bennetts and Skinners to the use of brother George during Philippa's lifetime. On her death they were to go to John Wood.
> (b) Manor of Ankerwicke to brother George and his heirs.
> (c) Manor of Theydon Mount to Philippa for life and afterwards to brother George and his heirs.
> (d) Leases of several properties in Fleet Street to John Wood.

Philippa was allowed to 'dispose at her will and pleasure' of all the goods that she had brought into the marriage, together with 700 ounces of his plate, which she must leave for her successor. All the furniture 'in my new building' and all at Mounthall was to go eventually to George. Smith directed that each successive owner of Theydon Mount should leave two-thirds of his property to his successor in the manor.

His legacies included:

> (a) 300 ounces of plate for the marriage of a niece.
> (b) A clever child, son of his servants, was to have five marks a year to keep him at Walden School and then to go up to Cambridge.
> (c) A gilt cup with the seven planets on it was for the Queen.
> (d) His physician was given the 'Monuments of Martyrs' in two volumes.
> (e) Henry Butler for faithful work with the stills was given the works of Chaucer.
> (f) All his Latin and Greek books (about 300) were to go to Queens' College, Cambridge, 'because I see that none of these which shall succeed me are learned'. The books were to be chained up or distributed amongst the fellows; 'my great globe of myne owne makinge' was also for Queens' College (Fig. 45). Smith's celestial globe is still displayed in Queens' Library.

In the spring of 1577 William Smith, his sister's son, died. William had been in Smith's service and was much valued. He had continued to farm in Walden the fields known as 'Bessel Ditches', which Smith's father had owned. It would appear that the 'Bessel Ditches' are the same as the 'Battle Ditches', so the fields would have been in the vicinity of the ditches, which partially circumscribe the town on its southern and western boundaries (Fig. 46).

Smith added a codicil that his widow be looked after and 'the children be provided for to be well brought up in the fear of God'.

Fig. 45. Thomas Smith globe in Library of Queens' College, Cambridge. This shows Sagittarius and other signs of the Zodiac. Smith made it from wood and used it for his astrological observations. At that time, there was much interest in the construction of terrestrial and celestial globes, stimulated by the maritime explorations of Francis Drake and others.

Fig. 46. The Battle Ditches at Saffron Walden, farmed by Smith's father and later his nephew.

References

1: The Lonely Boy

1. Strype, J., *The Life of the Learned Sir Thomas Smith Kt.* (1698, reprinted 1820), p. 3.
2. Allen, E., *Chepying Walden/Saffron Walden, 1438-90: A Small Town* (PhD thesis, 2011 unpub.)
3. Culliford, S.G., *William Strachey, 1572-1621* (1965), p.18f.
4. *A History of the County of Essex,* Vol. 2, pp. 110-115.
5. White, M., *Saffron Walden's History: A Chronological Compilation* (1991), p. 36.
6. Strype, *op.cit.,* p. 5.
7. Rowntree, C. B., *Saffron Walden Then and Now* (1951), p. 17.
8. Rowntree, *op.cit.* p. 17.
9. William Strachey (1493-1564), whose wife went by the delightful name of Amiable Bird, was a direct ancestor of Lytton Strachey (1880-1932), the critic and author of *Eminent Victorians*, and of Evelyn John Strachey (1901-68), the Labour Cabinet Minister.
10. Rowntree, *op.cit.*, p. 59.
11. Dewar, M., *Sir Thomas Smith: A Tudor Intellectual in Office* (1964). Dewar states that 'draper' can be used to describe a small sheep farmer. The authority for this is not stated, as this usage is not to be found in the Oxford English Dictionary. In a deed dated 13 March 1495/96 for a messuage abutting on to Castle Street, Saffron Walden, a John Smith is described as a 'barker', that is one who removes tree bark for use in tanning (see ERO D/B 2/1/38). In another deed dated 1511 concerning a shop in Butcher's Row, a Thomas Smyth (possibly the brother of John Smith, senior?) is mentioned along with Thomas Stracy the Elder of Walden (see ERO D/B 2/2/32).
12. Smith's Memoirs are held at the British Library (Additional Ms 48047/Sloane MS 25).
13. White, *op.cit.,* p.36. A large part of the Priory was taken down by a Mr Maurice. But the north part of the house with its living room and staircase, and the outside wall with its coping stones, are said to go back to Tudor times and may have formed part of a property occupied by a member of the Smith family. The author is grateful to the householder, Mrs Tessa Hawkes, for this information.
14. The preamble to the 1549-1550 accounts of Saffron Walden refers to the grant of privileges to the Treasurer, Chamberlains and the town, and the efforts of John Smith junior and Sir Thomas Smith, his brother, in securing these.
These same accounts refer to the expenditure of 'one pounde of saffron given to ye Queene's attorney' (1565-66, p. 65). See ERO T/A 401/2.
15. Strype states that Smith 'later advanced the school into a royal foundation, with a good endowment from the King in the third year of his reign, when he granted to the school a corn mill and a malt mill with its tolls and benefits and an annuity of twelve pounds, arising out of the manor of Willingale Spane in Essex'. There may be some confusion here as Johane Bradbury, when she obtained the school's charter in 1522 had agreed to pay the school an annual charge of £12 from her lands at Willingale near Ongar (see White, *op.cit.,* pp. 33-35).
16. See website www.damebradburys.com
17. Smith kept short autobiographical notes in Latin, which run for only seven pages, as well as detailed astrological notes (M.S. Addit. Brit. Mus. 325, f.2; Sloane M.S. 325).
G.M. Nicholls in 'Additions to the Biographies of Sir John Cheke and Sir Thomas Smith', *Archaeologia* xxxviii, sets out 'Autobiographical Notes of Sir Thomas Smith' (pp. 116-119) and provides an English translation, which he rendered in the third person (pp. 104-112), as well as some 'Other Notes from Sir Thomas Smith's Astrological Manuscript (pp. 119-120).

2: The Cambridge Scholar

1. Cited in Anderson, J.M., *The Honorable Burden of Public Office* (2010), pp. 56-57.
2. Preface to his translation of Martin Cortes' *The Arte of Nauigation* (1572); cited Anderson, *op.cit.,* p. 57.
3. Cited Anderson, *op.cit.,* p. 57.
4. Searle, E.G., *History of Queens' College, 1446-1560,* pp. 320f.
5. Anderson, *op.cit.,* p. 59.
6. Smith's Memoirs f.3 recto.
7. *Correspondence of Matthew Parker* (Parker Society, 1853) p. 36.
8. Smith's Memoirs f.3 recto.
9. Smith's Memoirs f.82 verso.

3: The Edwardian Secretary of State

1. Benet and colet were minor orders within the Catholic Church. They are mentioned in Caxton's *Chronicles of England*, 1520, as being one of four orders, namely benet, colet, deacon and priest. *Benet* seems to have been used in exorcisms and *colet* as a form of acolyte.
2. William Parr, the 1st Marquess of Northampton (1513-71), was the brother of Catherine Parr, the sixth wife of Henry VIII. William's first marriage to Anne Bourchie was annulled by Act of Parliament and Anne's children by her lover were declared bastards. Parr obtained his wife's lands and was created Earl of Essex. He later married Elizabeth Brooke. The marriage was declared valid in 1548, invalid in 1553, and valid again 1558, which shows how the law could be bent for political ends. Parr and his wife were leaders in the attempt to put Lady Jane Grey on the throne after the death of Edward VI. Parr was convicted of high treason, but shortly afterwards released.
3. Strype, *The Life of the Learned Sir Thomas Smith Kt.* (1698, reprinted 1820), p. 42.
4. Smith to the Duchess of Somerset, July/August 1549, BM Harleian Ms 6989, f.141. See G.M. Nicholls, 'Additions to the Biographies of Sir John Cheke and Sir Thomas Smith', *Archaeologia* xxxviii: 'Sir Thomas Smith's Defence of his Conduct and Character, addressed to the Duchess of Somerset, pp. 120-127.
5. Ryrie, A., *The Sorcerer's Tale: Faith and Fraud in Tudor England* (2008).
6. Dewar, M., *Sir Thomas Smith: A Tudor Intellectual in Office* (1964).
7. Dewar, *op.cit.,* p. 39.
8. Strype, *op.cit.,* p. 49.
9. Burning at the stake was very rare during Edward's reign. The only other instance that I can find was that carried out at Smithfield in 1551 on George Van Perris, a Dutch Arian, who in the contrary case to Joan Bocher denied the divinity of Christ.
10. See Foxe's *Acts and Monuments*, 1570, p. 1551.
11. See note 4.
12. Latimer, *Sermons* (Corrie, E. (Ed.) 1844, p. 122.
13. Wood, A., *The 1549 Rebellions and the Making of Modern Britain* (2007).
14. Smith, T., *The Treatise on the Wages of a Roman Soldier* (1562).
15. Smith to Cecil, 19 July 1549, Tytler, i.185.
16. See website http://mises.org/daily/4676
17. Strype, J., *Sir John Cheke* (1705), p. 40.
18. The book was attributed partly to one WS and partly to John Hales, but Mary Dewar and other scholars have firmly attributed the work to Smith.
19. See note 4.
20. Tytler, i. 209-10.

21. Tytler, i. 223.

22. Ken Neale points out (pers.comm.) that Wingfield was one of the Commissioners sent to Fotheringhay in February 1587 to inform Mary Stuart (Queen of Scots) of the decision to execute her. Most of them favoured judicial execution, but Wingfield was one of those who advocated assassination and was apparently prepared to do the deed himself.

23. B.M. Royal MS 17A xvii.

4: The Wilderness Years

1. This large house, which had 20 rooms, was pulled down after being partly destroyed by fire in the 18th century. Ankerwicke or Ankerwycke is the site of the famous Ankerwicke Yew, which is close to the ruins of St Mary's Priory, a Benedictine nunnery built in the 12th century. The yew is a male tree with a girth of eight metres (26 feet) at a height of 0.3 metres. Various estimates have put its age at between 2,000 and 2,500 years. The tree is said to have been the location for the signing of the Magna Carta in 1215, and also where Henry VIII met Anne Boleyn in the 1530s.

2. SP 12/251/118.

3. See website http://politicworm.com/oxford; 'Shakespeare's Tutor: Sir Thomas Smith', *The Oxfordian* Vol III (2000), pp. 19-44.

4. Smith to Cecil, 7 November 1562. SP 70/44/996/f. 776.

5. Strype, J., *The Life of the Learned Sir Thomas Smith Kt.* (1698, reprinted 1820), p. 67.

6. Strype, *op.cit.,* p. 60. This monument, like most of the medieval and Tudor monuments in Saffron Walden Parish Church, has long since been removed.

7. Elizabeth's distrust may have been connected with the sexual abuse that she suffered at the hands of Thomas Seymour and his wife, Catherine Parr. See Loades, D., *Elizabeth I: The Golden Age of Gloriana* (2003), p. 11.

8. Smith to Dudley, 12 October 1565. Historical Manuscripts Commission, box 67.

9. Smith to Elizabeth, 1 April 1563. S.P. 70/54/559.

5: The Elizabethan Envoy

1. Dewar, M., *Sir Thomas Smith: A Tudor Intellectual in Office* (1964), p. 102

2. Smith to Cecil, 13 April 1563, Forbes: *A Full View of the Public Transactions in the Reign of Elizabeth*, ii.386, cited Dewar, *op.cit.,* p. 95.

3. Elizabeth to Smith, 5 July 1563. SP70/60/975.

4. Smith to Cecil, 24 January 1564, SP 70/67/100, f. 79.

5. In England the mark never appeared as a coin but was used as a unit of account. Originally it was worth one pound but later was valued at 13s 8d, or two thirds of a pound.

6. Smith to Cecil, 11 May 1564, SP 70/71/338, f. 316.

7. Dewar, *op.cit.,* p. 105

8. BM Addit. MS. 35.831, f. 207.

9. Smith to Cecil, 16 April 1565. S.P. 70/77/1103, f.917.

10. See Neale, K., *An Elizabethan Salamander:* Kenneth Newton Lecture, 15 October 1998.

11. Hoby to Cecil, 16 May 1566. S.P. 70/84/387, f.318.

6: The Elizabethan Secretary of State

1. Nichols, J., *Progresses and Public Processions of Queen Elizabeth* (1823), i. p. 281.

2. See Strype, *The Life of the Learned Sir Thomas Smith Kt.* (1698, reprinted 1820). Chap. XI.

3. Smith to Heneage, 6 November 1570. *Hist. MSS. Comm.*, lxxi. 12-13.

4. This was the bull *Regnans in Excelsis* in which Pope Pius V declared Elizabeth a heretic and released her subjects from all allegiance to her.

5. In 1565 Mary married Henry Stuart, Lord Darnley. In February 1567 Darnley was murdered by conspirators, led probably by James Hepburn, Earl Bothwell. In May 1567 Mary married Bothwell, arousing suspicions that she had been party to the murder of Darnley. The Scottish lords forced Mary to abdicate in favour of her son, James, King of England 1603-25. Mary escaped from Loch Leven Castle and made her way to England. She was finally executed at Fotheringhay Castle, Northamptonshire on 8 February 1587.

6. Smith and Killigrew to Elizabeth, 8 January 1572. Cal. SP Foreign 1572-74, no. 20.

7. Strype, *op.cit.,* p. 140.

8. Elizabeth to Smith and Wilson, 15 Sept. 1571. BM. MS. Cotton Caligula, C.iii, f.229, pr. H Ellis, *Original Letters,* ser. I, ii, 261.

9. *Historical Manuscripts Commission, Hatfield,* i.no. 1609.

10. Instructions to Smith on departing to France. BM Addit. MS 4109ff., 49-60.

11. Smith to Elizabeth, 5 January 1572. *Cal. SP. Foreign,* 1572-1574, no. 8.

12. Smith to Lady Elizabeth, 9 January 1572. SP 70/146/415.

13. Smith to Sir James Croft, 9 January 1572, SP 70/146/414.

14. Smith to Burghley, Good Friday, 1572. BM Cotton MS. Vespasian, F. vi.16.

15. Smith to Lady Philippa, 17 May 1572. SP 70/146/490.

16. Smith to Lady Philippa, 22 April 1572. SP 70/146/478.

17. Dewar, *Sir Thomas Smith: A Tudor Intellectual in Office* (1964), p. 171.

18. Strype, *op.cit.,* p. 94.

19. Smith to Burghley, 13 March 1574. B.M. Landsdowne MS. 19/86.

20. Smith to Walsingham, 27 July 1572. BM Cotton MS. Vespasian F vi, No. 117.

21. Smith to Walsingham, 11 January 1572. BM Cotton MS. Vespasian F vi 79, No. 228.

22. Smith to Burghley, 12 February 1573, B.M. Landsdowne MS. 16/42, f. 86.

23. Smith to Cecil, 7 March 1563. SP 70/52/411.

24. Smith to Walsingham, 26 September 1572. BM Harleian MS. 260/188.

25. Smith to Burghley, 5 May 1574, B.M. Landsdowne MS. 19/39.

26. Smith to Burghley, 7 March 1575, B.M. Harleian MS 6999/62.

27. Smith to Burghley, 22 April 1576, B.M. Harleian MS 6992/20, f. 39.

28. Smith to Thynne, 31 May 1576. *Wilts Arch. and Nat. Hist. Mag., xviii* (1878), 266. The MS is at Longleat.

29. Rowntree, C.B. *Saffron Walden: Then and Now* (1951), p. 9, asserts that Harvey was a cousin of Smith and lived next door to 'the Smyth mansion in Walden Market Place'.

30. Nashe, T., *Strange Newes* (1593).

7: The Merchant Venturer

1. Smith to Burghley, 8 February 1572, S.P. 70/146/428.

2. Smith to Cecil, 6 June 1565. SP 70/78/1228, f. 1007.

3. Smith to Cecil, 7 November 1565. SP 70/81/1654, f.1302.

4. Quinn, D.B., 'Sir Thomas Smith and the beginnings of English colonial theory', *Proc. Amer. Philos. Soc.* LXXXIX (1945).

5. Smith to his son, 5 April 1572. SP 70/146/456.

6. Smith to his son, 8 May 1572. SP 70/146/482.

7. Smith to John Wood, 8 May 1572. SP 70/146/491.

8. Maginn, C. ODNB 2004 online edn Jan2008 http://www.oxforddnb.com/view/article/69171.

9. ERO D/DSh/01/7, 20 December 1573.

8: The Lasting Legacy

1. Pevsner, N., *The Buildings of England: Essex* (1954), pp. 353-5.
2. See Drury, P.J., A Fayre House, Buylt by Sir Thomas Smith: The Development of Hill Hall, Essex, 1557-81', *Journal of the British Archaeological Association*, Vol. CXXXVI (1983), p.118: 'Hill Hall is one of a small group of major buildings of *c*.1540-75 in which classical elements largely derived from early French renaissance architecture and decoration were combined in varying proportions with the Tudor Gothic tradition. One of the first was Lacock Abbey (Wilts.) remodelled by Sir William Sharington in 1540-9. Sharington was associated with Lord Protector Somerset, who was responsible for … Old Somerset House in London of *c*.1547-52, whose Strand front was perhaps the first attempt at a coherent classical façade in England. Its construction was supervised by Sir John Thynne, who from 1554 was building on his own account at Longleat (Wilts)'. See also Drury, P. & Simpson, R., *Hill Hall: A Singular House devised by a Tudor Intellectual* (2009). See also Neale, K., 'Sir Thomas Smith and Hill Hall, Essex', *Essex Journal* 5/1 (1970) and 6/1 (1971).
3. Strype informs us that in the dining room in the west window were painted emblems of four of the seven deadly sins. Around fornication or porneia 'is a set of fiddlers, under a ladies window serenading her, and a woman naked appearing at the window, throwing water out of a chamberpot upon their heads' (*op.cit.*, p. 230). These windows were painted in 1569. There is a tradition in the house that some of the paintings in the house were done by Sir Thomas' own hand in 1568, but Anne Padfield, Hill Hall Steward (pers.comm.) thinks not, commenting: 'The Cupid and Psyche paintings are copies of engravings which Smith possessed in his library, and which seem to have inspired some of the architectural elements of the house. The Old Testament scenes (Ahaz and Hezekiah) are not copies from known sources, except for one panel. The quality of the painting is better and more original.'
4. Drury & Simpson, *op.cit.*, (2009), p. 260.
5. See Drury & Simpson, *op.cit.*
6. Its most famous inmate was the call-girl, Christine Keeler, a central figure in the Profumo affair.
7. Drury, *op.cit.* (1983), p. 113: 'In his annalistic autobiography (written in Latin), Smith translated "Hill Hall" as "Montisaula". This he often anglicised to "Mont[e] Hall" as an alternative to "Hill Hall". Both are used indiscriminately in his will, as is the phrase, "this house of Monte Hall or Hill Hall", and the imprecise usage is carried over into the records of the 1601 Chancery cause which stemmed from the will. Many of his letters are dated at "Monthall".' It was this confusion that led Mrs Dewar to the unlikely conclusion that Smith built two great houses on the Theydon Mount estate.
8. Prerogative Court of Canterbury, PCC 31 Daughtry.
9. ERO Q/SR, Cal. Session Rolls, Essex vii, 1576-1577.
10. Strype, *op.cit.*, pp. 203-204.
11. There is a handsome portrait of a red-bearded man said to be Sir Thomas Smith, which hangs in the dining hall at Queens' Cambridge behind the high table. However Dewar asserts (p. 211) that this portrait is now known to be that of 'Customer' Smyth. Thomas 'Customer' Smythe (*c.* 1522-1591) was the collector of custom duties ('customer') in London during the Elizabethan period. Confusingly he had a son and namesake Sir Thomas Smythe who was an active supporter of the Virginia Colony.

Note re portraits, p. 57

There are a number of portraits of Sir Thomas Smith, including the framed portrait that formerly hung in Hill Hall, and copies of this portrait which hang in Saffron Walden Town Hall, the Middle Temple and Eton College. However, Kenneth Neale has concluded that none of the existing portraits can be positively identified as being authentic representations of Sir Thomas Smith; he considers that the effigy of Smith in Theydon Mount Church, devised by Smith himself, may be the most reliable and likely portrayal of Smith. See Kenneth Neale: 'Sir Thomas Smith of Hill Hall: An Iconography,' in *Essex Journal*, Volume Six, 1971, pp. 17-22.

Bibliography

Primary Sources

British Library: Smith Memoirs (Additional Ms 48047/Sloane MS 25).
British Museum (B.M.): MS. Addit. MS; Cotton MS' Harleian MS; Landsdowne
Essex Record Office (ERO): Calendars of Session Rolls; D/B 2/; D/DSh/01/7; T/A 401/2.
State Papers (SP): Cal. SP Foreign. Letters of Sir Thomas Smith.
Historical Manuscripts Commission, *Hatfield*.
Prerogative Court of Canterbury 1383-1858, 31 Daughtry (now at National Archives).

Published Sources

Page, W. & Round, H. (Eds), *Victoria History of the County of Essex*, Vol 2 (1907).
Allen, E., *Chepying Walden/Saffron Walden, 1438-90: A Small Town* (PhD thesis unpub., 2011).
Anderson, J.M., *The Honorable Burden of Public Office* (2010).
Archer, I., *The Oxford Dictionary of National Biography* (2004-10).
Correspondence of Matthew Parker (1853).
Corrie, E. (Ed.), *Latimer, Sermons* (1844).
Cortes, M., *The Arte of Nauigation* (1572).
Culliford. S.G., *William Strachey, 1572-1621* (1965).
Danielsson, B., *Sir Thomas Smith: Literary and Linguistic Works* (1963).
Dewar, M., *Sir Thomas Smith: A Tudor Intellectual in Office* (1964). Saffron Walden Town Library, E.SAFF.920. The author is greatly indebted to Mary Dewar upon whose industry and scholarship he has drawn extensively in this work.
Dewar, M. (Ed.), *De Republica Anglorum by Sir Thomas Smith* (1982).
Drury P.J., 'A Fayre House, Buylt by Sir Thomas Smith: The Development of Hill Hall, Essex, 1557-81', *Journal of the British Archaeological Association*, Vol. CXXXVI (1983).
Drury, P. & Simpson, R., *Hill Hall: A Singular House devised by a Tudor Intellectual* (2009).
Emmison, F.G., *Tudor Secretary* (1961).
Foxe's *Acts and Monuments* (1570).
Granger, J., *History of England with Portraits,* A 150C Vol 3.
Loades, D., *Elizabeth 1: The Golden Reign of Gloriana* (2003).
Neale, J.E., *Queen Elizabeth* (1934).
Neale, K., 'Sir Thomas Smith and Hill Hall, Essex', *Essex Journal* Vol 5/1 (1970), 6/1 (1971); 'Sir Thomas Smith of Hill Hall: An Iconography,' *Essex Journal*, Vol 6 (1971).
Neale, K., *An Elizabethan Salamander:* Kenneth Newton Lecture (1998).
Neale, K., *Saint Michael the Archangel, Theydon Mount: an appreciation historical and architectural* (1973).
Nicholls, J.G., 'Some additions to the biography of Sir Thomas Smith', *Archaeologia* XXVIII, 98-127 (1860).
Nichols, J., *Progresses and Public Processions of Queen Elizabeth* (1823).
Pevsner, N., *The Buildings of England: Essex* (1954).
Quinn, D.B. 'Sir Thomas Smith and the beginnings of English colonial theory', *Proc. Amer. Philos. Soc.* LXXIX (1945).
Rowntree, C.B., *Saffron Walden Then and Now* (1951).
Ryrie, A.. *The Sorcerer's Tale: Faith and Fraud in Tudor England* (2008).
Searle, W.G., *History of Queens' College, 1446-1560* (1867).
Smith, T., *Discourse of the Commonweal* (1549).

Smith, T., *De Republica Anglorum* (1562-65 – pub. 1583).
Strype, J., *The Life of the Learned Sir Thomas Smith Kt.* (1698, reprinted 1820).
Strype, J., *Sir John Cheke* (1705).
Tytler , P.F., *England under the Reigns of Edward VI and Mary* (1839).
Wiltshire Archaeological & Natural History Magazine (1878). MS at Longleat.
White, M., *Saffron Walden's History: A Chronological Compilation* (1991).
Wood, A., *The 1549 Rebellions and the Making of Modern Britain* (2007).

Websites

http://www.oxforddnb.com/view/article/25906;/article/69171.
http://mises.org/daily/4676
www.damebradburys.com
http://politicworm.com/oxford; *The Oxfordian* Vol III 2000 – 'Shakespeare's Tutor: Sir Thomas Smith'.

INDEX